JIM BURNS

90 Days

THROUGH THE

New Testament

DEVELOPING A 20-MINUTE DAILY TIME WITH GOD

Regal Books

A Division of Gospel Light
Ventura, California, U.S.A.

Published by Regal Books
A Division of Gospel Light
Ventura, California, U.S.A.
Printed in U.S.A.

Regal Books is a ministry of Gospel Light, an evangelical Christian publisher dedicated to serving the local church. We believe God's vision for Gospel Light is to provide church leaders with biblical, user-friendly materials that will help them evangelize, disciple and minister to children, youth and families.

It is our prayer that this Regal Book will help you discover biblical truth for your own life and help you meet the needs of others. May God richly bless you.

For a free catalog of resources from Regal Books/Gospel Light please contact your Christian supplier or call 1-800-4-GOSPEL.

Scripture quotations are taken from the *NIV*—The Holy Bible, *New International Version,* Copyright © 1973, 1978, 1984 International Bible Society. Used by permission of Zondervan Bible Publishers.

Library of Congress Cataloging-in-Publication Data

Burns, Jim, 1953–
90 days through the New Testament: developing a 20 minute daily time with God / Jim Burns.
    p.   cm.
    Includes bibliographical references.
    Summary: A daily devotional book dividing the New Testament into ninety separate readings, accompanied by questions and background information for each book of the New Testament.
    ISBN 0-8307-1456-1
    1. Bible. N.T.–Devotional use–Juvenile literature. 2. Children–Prayer books and devotions–English [1. Bible. N.T.–Study. 2. Prayer books and devotions.] I. Title. II. Title: Ninety days through the New Testament.
BS2341.3B87   1990   90-41243
242'.2-dc20   CIP
                                              AC

6 7 8 9 10 11 12 13 14 15 16 17 / 02 01 00 99 98 97 96 95

Any omission of credits is unintentional. The publisher requests documentation for future printings.

Rights for publishing this book in other languages are contracted by Gospel Literature International (GLINT). GLINT also provides technical help for the adaptation, translation, and publishing of Bible study resources and books in scores of languages worldwide. For further information, contact GLINT, Post Office Box 4060, Ontario, California, 91761-1003, U.S.A., or the publisher.

To two of the most wonderful churches in the world: First Presbyterian Orange and South Coast Community Church. You have brought me affirmation, lifelong friendship, and true fulfillment.

Special thanks to:

Pete Albright	Daryl Pfischner
Michelle Bath	Craig Sanders
Bill Bower	Pam Sears
Del Burnett	Terry Sherry
Barb Connell	Katie Smith
Mike Driggs	Todd Temple
Doug Fields	Donna Van Haren
Donna Gibson	Doug Webster
Lisa Hanson	Gary Webster
Rick Larsh	Robin Webster
Gary Lenhart	Bernie Yonkers
Sydney Perry	

My deepest appreciation and love to the intern youth staff, past and present. Thank you for your many lessons on life. I am most blessed for having worked and lived alongside you.

CONTENTS

- The Challenge
- Getting Started
- Introduction to the New Testament

THE 90-DAY EXPERIENCE

THE GOSPELS

THE ACTS OF THE APOSTLES

LETTERS

REVELATION

THE CHALLENGE

If you are anything like I am, at times you struggle with setting aside the quality, consistent devotional time it takes to get better acquainted with God. One evening in the frustration of not meeting with God as often as I wanted to and feeling like I needed to get a better understanding of Scripture, I put together a personal Bible study and devotional program for myself to follow. My goals were to read through the New Testament in a disciplined daily way within a three-month period of time.

Each day I set aside approximately 20 minutes to read a portion of Scripture, reflect and pray, and then respond to God and grow. This three-month experiment in faith was the single most effective program of spiritual growth and discipline I have ever experienced. I needed the motivation and structure to make a daily time with God a habit.

My challenge to you who desire unlimited growth in your Christian faith—but sometimes fail to discipline your times with God—is to begin today a three-month process of making your time with God disciplined. You will not be the same person three months from now. This little devotional book can be the stimulus toward developing a daily meeting with God for the rest of your life.

Twenty minutes a day is not a great deal of time when we think of the important growth that will transform our lives as we spend time in God's Word. As you consider the challenge of the 90-Day Experience, keep in mind the powerful words in 1 Peter 1:24: "All men are like grass, and all their glory is like the flowers of the field. The grass withers and the flower falls, *but the word of the Lord stands forever.*"

—Jim Burns
Dana Point, California

GETTING STARTED

A disciplined daily devotional life is not an option for Christian growth. It's a must! And it's also a privilege. You have the opportunity every day to spend time with your Creator and Savior. This daily quiet time with God will transform your life like nothing else can.

Let me explain what you will find in this book. You'll get a brief introduction of each book in the New Testament. Sometimes understanding who wrote the book and who they were writing to will make a big difference in understanding the important themes and highlights of each book in the New Testament.

Having read through the overview you will be ready to explore each book in the New Testament. The daily format is simple. Here's how it works:

- *Read and Answer* questions are straightforward questions about facts. Occasionally they will prompt you to read between the lines for significant points.

- *Reflect and Pray* questions suggest a topic for your own life. You, too, will be able to say with David, "Your word is a lamp to my feet and a light for my path" (Psalm 119:105).

- *Respond and Grow* questions give you the opportunity to put into practice the truths you learn each day.

Let me encourage you to approach your daily times in the Bible with a sense of expectation. Expect to meet Jesus in a new way each day. Expect God to speak to you in a very personal way. And expect to become the person God wants you to be as you daily spend time in His Word. Claim the promise of James: "Draw near to God and He will draw near to you" (4:8 *NASB*). Below are some important thoughts on how your devotional time can be made more meaningful.

Find a specific time each day to meet with God. If you get in the habit of meeting with God at a specific time without interruptions, it will be easier to remain faithful to this commitment.

Find a quiet place to meet with God. Where you meet with God is important. Wherever you choose, make sure that it is free from distractions.

Determine what you hope to accomplish during your meeting with God. In other words, have a method. Do not approach your quiet time in a helter-skelter manner. Let 90 DAYS THROUGH THE NEW TESTAMENT serve as a program for your time with God.

Remember that a devotional meeting with God is not in-depth Bible study. A devotional time with God should include Bible reading, but not necessarily in-depth Bible study. Also save time for these things:

Praise: "Let everything that has breath praise the Lord" (Psalm 150:6). Tell God of His greatness and His majestic power. Adore the Lord of lords and King of kings.

Thanksgiving: "Give thanks in all circumstances, for this is God's will for you in Christ Jesus" (1 Thessalonians 5:18). No matter what your situation or what problem you are facing, take time to consider the things in your life for which you can be thankful. This thankfulness can help you overcome negative thoughts and emotions.

Confession: "If we confess our sins, he is faithful and just and will forgive us our sins and purify us from all unrighteousness" (1 John 1:9). We keep communication with God open when we confess our sins to Him. The word "confession" comes from a root word meaning "to agree together with." When you confess your sins to God, you are simply agreeing with Him that you have fallen short of the way He wants you to live. You are letting Him know that you desire a right relationship with Him.

Petition: "Ask and it will be given to you; seek and you will find; knock and the door will be opened to you" (Matthew 7:7). This is an important part of your prayer life, but it is not the only part. Too often we rush to God, ask for things, and then rush away. Do pray for your family, friends, church, government, and yourself. Do not be afraid to ask God for things, but remember who is the Lord in the relationship—God is, not you.

Listening: "My son, if you accept my words and store up my commands within you, turning your ear to wisdom and applying your heart to understanding....Then you will understand the fear of the Lord and find the knowledge of God" (Proverbs 2:1,5). Prayer is two-way communication. When you pray, take time to listen. God is speaking to you. Write down the thoughts which come to mind. Then test those thoughts through the inner witness of your spirit. Take time to be quiet before the Lord.

Now grab a copy of the Bible (I've used the *New International Version* here), this manual, and a pencil—and enjoy the adventure.

INTRODUCTION TO THE NEW TESTAMENT

As you begin to read the New Testament, it is important for you to know how it is put together. The New Testament is composed of 27 books, and these books are divided into four categories—the Gospels, the Acts of the Apostles, the Epistles (or letters), and Revelation.

THE GOSPELS

- "Gospel" means "good news"; Matthew, Mark, Luke, and John are the four accounts of the good news of Jesus Christ. Although never meant to be a complete biography, these books do tell the most important events and teachings in the life of Jesus. Together the four portraits, each highlighting different aspects of the character of Jesus, offer a dynamic and compelling picture of Jesus of Nazareth, the Son of God and our Savior.

THE ACTS OF THE APOSTLES

- The section after the gospels is the Acts of the Apostles. This book is filled with the history of the early church after the death and resurrection of Jesus. Most of this section deals with the lives and ministries of Paul and Peter. This is a thrilling section to read as you witness the rapid expansion of the early church.

LETTERS

- Next come the 21 New Testament books which are written in the form of letters. These epistles are a more personal means of communication, as the writers address specific congregations or individuals for the purpose of encouragement and teaching. These letters fall into two main groups: those which Paul wrote, and those written by other people.

REVELATION

- Finally, the book of Revelation is a fascinating piece of literature much different from the other books in the New Testament. This book is apocalyptic in style: It is poetic and visionary, communicating ideas through symbols and imagery. To take this picture-language literally or to treat the book as a logical timetable is to go against the entire spirit of it. This book, while rooted in the Old Testament, is dominated by the person of the victorious Christ.

Jesus as Messiah King

Above his head they placed the written charge against him:
THIS IS JESUS, THE KING OF THE JEWS (Matthew 27:37).

THE GOSPEL ACCORDING TO MATTHEW

- Who is this Jesus of Nazareth?
- How does He fit with the Messiah spoken of by the Hebrew prophets?
- What guidelines does Jesus offer for life?

John 20:31 states the purpose of that gospel as well as of the other three: "These are written that you may believe that Jesus is the Christ, the Son of God, and that by believing you may have life in his name"—a purpose as crucial to us as to people in the time of the gospel writers. The same issue is at stake: Belief will lead to eternal life, unbelief to eternal death. Therefore, the two worlds are alike: Twenty centuries later we should ask with the first-century believers, "Who is this Jesus of Nazareth?"

Matthew, a Jewish Christian, writes specifically to Jewish readers to answer this question and support his claim that Jesus is the fulfillment of Jewish prophecy. Matthew's purpose seems to be education rather than evangelism—he wrote not for the outsider but in order that believers could deepen their understanding of their roots.

In the very first verse, Matthew introduces Jesus as the "son of David" and so begins his apologetic: Jesus is clearly presented as the Messiah long awaited by the nation of Israel. Matthew quotes again and again from the Old Testament as he argues that Jesus is the One spoken of in the prophecies, that He is the fulfillment of the law, and that He is in fact the "King of the Jews" promised by God long ago.

The organization of the gospel reflects Matthew's purpose: Five blocks of teaching are linked by narrative. As you read the book of Matthew, pay particular attention to these five distinguishing characteristics:

1. Matthew's sensitivity to his Jewish audience
2. His great interest in the end of the age and the Second Coming of Christ
3. Teaching about the life of the Christian community and Christian fellowship
4. The five main blocks of teaching (these are italicized in the outline in the Appendix)
5. Emphasis on Christ as King

DAY 1

☐ **Matthew 1–4**

READ AND ANSWER

Note how many times Matthew refers to Old Testament prophecies in these four chapters. Keep a list or tally as you read through this gospel.

1: ㉓ Isa 7:14
2: ① Mic 5:1 ³ Gen 49:10
⑬ Num 24:8 ⁸ Hosea 11:1
⑰ Jer 31:15
3: ③ Isa 40:3

4: ④ Duet 8:3
⑥ Po 91:11, 12
⑦ Duet 6:16
⑩ Duet 6:13 10:20
⑮ Isa 9:1, 2

(4:17) Comment on the fact that the temptation in the wilderness preceded the beginning of Jesus' preaching ministry. Do you think this ordering is significant? Why or why not?

Show Jesus as the Son of God.
Empowered Him w/strength + energy we do not see.

REFLECT AND PRAY

(1:23) What is the meaning of "Immanuel"? To what extent is God with you in your daily life? *God w/us   Holy Spirit*

(4:19) When did Jesus first call you to follow Him? Thank Him for preparing you to respond to His call. Thank Him for differences He has made in your life.

RESPOND AND GROW

(3:17) What is one thing you can do today that will make God the Father "well pleased" with you? *Obedience*

What idea, verse, or phrase can change my experience today?

memorize scripture to quote as Jesus did

15

DAY 2

☐ **Matthew 5–7**

READ AND ANSWER

These chapters comprise Jesus' most famous block of teaching, the Sermon on the Mount. What are five topics He deals with?

(7:24-27)   What are you building your life on? What is your most important goal or priority? Is that thing rock or sand?

REFLECT AND PRAY

(6:25-34)   This passage—one of the most beautiful and encouraging in Scripture—is summarized in verse 33.

• What is making you anxious today?

• What does Jesus teach here about your worries?

• How can you be seeking God's kingdom more persistently?

(7:1-11)   Consider your life in light of these verses. What have you hesitated to ask God for? How does this passage influence your prayers?

RESPOND AND GROW

(7:12)   Read this important verse again and fill in the blank: Today I will treat _____ as I want to be treated by _____.

What idea, verse, or phrase can change my experience today?

_____

_____

_____

DAY 3

READ AND ANSWER

(10:1-42)   What is the main point of this block of teaching? Answer this question by giving this chapter a title.

(10:1-42)   Consider the specifics of Christ's instructions. What assignment does He make, what warnings does He give, and what comfort does He offer?

REFLECT AND PRAY

(8:5-13; 9:20-22)   Think about the relationship between God's mighty power and our faith. How do these two things work together? What do these two examples of faith teach you about yourself?

RESPOND AND GROW

(8:23-27)   What storm in your life has Jesus calmed? What current turbulence can you ask Him to silence now?

What idea, verse, or phrase can change my experience today?

_____

_____

_____

☐ **Matthew 11–13**

READ AND ANSWER

(Are you keeping track of the references to Old Testament prophecies and their fulfillment in Jesus?)

(12:1-14)   Jesus claims that He is Lord of the Sabbath.

- How do the Pharisees react to this statement?

- How does Jesus' claim affect the man with the shriveled hand?

(12:46-50)   What tone of voice do you imagine Jesus used in verse 48? What does Jesus mean by His comments here?

REFLECT AND PRAY

(13:18-23)   What kind of ground did the seed of God's Word find in your life? If the farming conditions have changed through the years, comment on the difference. Spend some time talking to God about the growing conditions—past and present—in your life.

RESPOND AND GROW

(11:28-30)   What burden is making you weary? What is the yoke that Jesus offers you? You are free to make this trade today!

What idea, verse, or phrase can change my experience today?

_____

_____

_____

DAY 5

READ AND ANSWER

(14:1-22)   Imagine that day and its schedule of demanding activities.

- What had Jesus done that day?

- What did He do at the end of that long day?

- What do you usually do after a long and exhausting day?

- Work this week on following Christ's example: End each day with some time for prayer.

(15:21-28)   How did you react to Jesus' initial response to the woman's plea for help? What are your thoughts about her response to Jesus? What is the lesson from this story that you can apply to your life?

(16:24-26)   What does the phrase "take up his cross" mean to you?

REFLECT AND PRAY

(14:25-33)   Think back on a time when you took your eyes off Jesus and fell. Thank Jesus for catching you.

RESPOND AND GROW

(16:5-12)   What do you think Jesus felt when He heard the disciples' words in verse 7? What was Christ trying to tell them? Do you think you always understand God's message to you? What can you do today to hear Him more clearly?

What idea, verse, or phrase can change my experience today?

_____

_____

_____

DAY 6

☐ **Matthew 17–19**

READ AND ANSWER

(17:20,21) What does the mini-parable of these verses teach you about your faith? (The prayer of Mark 9:24 may be appropriate for you right now!)

(18:19,20) What do these two verses teach about prayer? About the importance of a community of believers?

REFLECT AND PRAY

(18:21-35) Look at yourself for a moment.

- For what has God forgiven you?

- Have you forgiven people who have hurt you or disappointed you?

- Are you an unmerciful servant who has been forgiven much but will not forgive little?

- Talk to God about the issue of forgiveness in your life.

RESPOND AND GROW

(19:16-30) What keeps the young man from having eternal life? What things in your life tend to keep you from loving Jesus wholeheartedly? Claim the promise of verse 19:26 for yourself.

What idea, verse, or phrase can change my experience today?

_____

_____

_____

DAY 7

READ AND ANSWER

(20:1-16)   What qualities of God's character does this parable reveal? What human characteristics stand in sharp contrast to the nature of God?

(22:34-40)   What are the motives of the Pharisees as they ask their questions? What lessons does Jesus teach in response to their questioning?

REFLECT AND PRAY

(21:12-17)   What does this episode suggest about the human aspects of Jesus Christ? Consider, for instance, His physical build and temperament.

RESPOND AND GROW

(20:26-28)   These verses point out another contrast between God's ways and human ways.

- How did Christ serve?

- How can you serve someone today at home? At school? At work?

What idea, verse, or phrase can change my experience today?

_____

_____

_____

☐ **Matthew 23–25**

READ AND ANSWER

(Be aware of Old Testament prophecies that Jesus is fulfilling!)

(23:27,28)   These verses come in the middle of Jesus' sharply-worded evaluation of the lifestyle and religious practices of the Sadducees and Pharisees.

- Give this outburst of righteous anger a title.

- How are you a "whitewashed tomb"? What needs to be cleaned from inside your heart?

(25:1-13)   What differentiates the wise from the foolish virgins?

REFLECT AND PRAY

(24:36-44)   Why doesn't Jesus give us specific information about when He will return? If you knew that He would come back next Thursday, how would you live differently between now and then?

(25:14-30)   With what things have you been entrusted? To what degree are you using them? To what purpose?

RESPOND AND GROW

(25:31-46)   Look around. Do you see hungry, thirsty, naked, or sad people? Make a firm resolution to meet the needs of someone this week and so minister *for* and *to* Christ.

What idea, verse, or phrase can change my experience today?

_____

_____

_____

DAY 9

READ AND ANSWER

(27:50-54)   What signs show that God is still at work in the crucifixion? Research the significance of the torn curtain (v. 51).

(27:62-64)   What do the chief priests and Pharisees mean by "the last deception" and "the first"? What are they concerned about?

REFLECT AND PRAY

(26:6-16)   Contrast the woman at Bethany with Judas Iscariot. What do they do? What are their motives? How do you love Jesus? How do you betray Him?

(28:16-20)   What is Jesus' last command to His people? What promise accompanies the command? How are you responding to the command? When have you claimed the promise?

RESPOND AND GROW

(26:31-35,69-75)   When have you, like Peter, made vows of loyalty to Jesus and then broken them by your actions or words? How did you deal with your stumbling?

What idea, verse, or phrase can change my experience today?

_____

_____

_____

Jesus as Servant

---

*For even the Son of Man did not come to be served, but to
serve, and to give his life as a ransom for many* (Mark 10:45).

THE GOSPEL ACCORDING TO MARK

- Who can overcome the powers of the world?
- How will the strength necessary to overcome these things be manifested?

One of Mark's favorite words is "immediately"—it occurs over forty
times in the sixteen chapters of this gospel. In this shortest of the four
gospels, Jesus is a man on the move. He has come as an invader of a fallen
planet which is wrongly impressed by power—be it Roman oppression,
financial clout, or nuclear madness.

Jesus Christ has come into this lost world as a person of inexhaustible
and divine strength: 70 percent of the book deals with miracles that Jesus
performed. Mark also shows us Jesus' tender side as well as His masterful
teaching ability. Between wondrously healing the sick and feeding the
hungry, Jesus takes time to bless and hold the children close to Him. He
also teaches important lessons about the kingdom of God with the parables of the sower, the lamp, and the mustard seed. Three times Jesus
predicts the passion which will surround His death.

Jesus Christ, God's Son and our Savior, is a man of genuine power which
comes from God and which manifests itself in working His will. As you
read the gospel of Mark, note the following:

1. Jesus as God's powerful man on the move
2. Jesus as God's conquering Son
3. People's responses to Jesus
4. Jesus' teachings on discipleship
5. The context of the three Passion predictions

☐ **Mark 1–3**

READ AND ANSWER

(1:1-45)   How many chapters did Matthew use to discuss the events of Mark 1? (This is the gospel of "immediately"!)

(2:1-5)   Whose faith does Jesus notice in this healing of the paralytic? What does this say to you about the importance of the Christian community?

(3:20-30)   What views of Jesus Christ are expressed here? Who holds these views? How is the view of the teachers of the law illogical?

REFLECT AND PRAY

(1:17,18)   In what area of your life is Jesus saying, "Follow me"? What is keeping you from responding as Simon and Andrew did?

RESPOND AND GROW

(1:35)   Note the quiet moment here between the healings, gathering of disciples, and teachings. What does this teach you about your busyness and your time for prayer?

What idea, verse, or phrase can change my experience today?

_____

_____

_____

DAY 11

☐ **Mark 4–6**

READ AND ANSWER

(4:10-12,21-23)   Why does Jesus speak in parables? How is the truth of a parable both hidden and revealed?

What qualities of Christ do Mark's accounts of His miracles bring into focus for you?

REFLECT AND PRAY

(4:24,25)   In light of what you're doing with what you read in the Bible, are verses 24 and 25 a promise you welcome or a warning you fear?

(6:34-44)   Jesus fed 5000 hungry people with five loaves and two fish. What personal and practical needs do you want to bring before Him today? Spend some time in prayer.

RESPOND AND GROW

(4:3-9,13-20)   Parable of the Sower: What can you do to make your life "good soil" which will accept the Word of God and bear fruit?

What idea, verse, or phrase can change my experience today?

_____

_____

_____

DAY 12

READ AND ANSWER

(8:29)   How do you answer Christ's question to Peter: "But who do you say that I am?" Jesus commanded Peter and the disciples not to share with anyone their knowledge of who He is. What does Christ command you to do with the knowledge? (See Matthew 28:18-20.) Are you being obedient?

REFLECT AND PRAY

(7:14-23)   What discussion preceded this message to the crowd? Which of the things Jesus mentions come out of you and reveal some uncleanness in your heart? Talk to God about these things.

(8:11-13)   In chapter 8, the Pharisees were seeking for a sign from heaven. Perhaps signs no longer come from heaven, but consider the past week. How has God revealed Himself to be a real part of your life?

(9:24)   Imagine the emotions behind this desperate father's cry. Have you ever shared his feelings or echoed his cry? How has God helped you overcome your unbelief?

RESPOND AND GROW

(9:35)   Jesus teaches that "If any one would be first, he must be last of all and servant of all" (Revised Standard Version). How was Jesus servant of all? How can you be a servant to someone today?

What idea, verse, or phrase can change my experience today?

_____

_____

_____

☐ **Mark 10–12**

READ AND ANSWER

(12:1-12)   What is Jesus' message in this parable of the tenants? Why, in your opinion, does this story cause the priests to plan to arrest Jesus?

(12:28-34)   What is the great commandment which Jesus shares with a questioning scribe? Why is obedience to this two-part commandment more important to Jesus than burnt offerings and sacrifices?

REFLECT AND PRAY

(11:15-19)   Jesus cleanses the temple at Jerusalem. He overturns the tables of the money-changers and the chairs of those selling pigeons. Why did He do this? What might Jesus want to overturn in your life to cleanse it? Will you let Him?

(12:41-44)   Why does Jesus approve of the widow's offering of two coins? Are you giving willingly out of your poverty? Are you giving generously out of your wealth?

RESPOND AND GROW

(10:17-31)   This conversation between Jesus and a rich young ruler serves as an example to His disciples and to us about the peril of riches. Which of your riches (material possessions, friends, goals, talents) might be standing between you and God? What are you going to do about this barrier?

What idea, verse, or phrase can change my experience today?

_____

_____

_____

DAY 14

READ AND ANSWER

(13:12,13)   Have you seen families divided over the issue of Jesus Christ? How do you think God feels about this?

(14:53-65; 15:1-5)   Look again at the way Jesus stood before Caiaphas and Pilate. What do you admire about Jesus? What puzzles you about His behavior?

REFLECT AND PRAY

(14:32-42)   Has there been a time in your life when you felt like Jesus in Gethsemane, when you cried to God and felt forsaken by Him? Talk to God about that time. How did that time affect your relationship with Him? What did you learn about God, your Father? What did you learn about yourself?

(15:39)   What moved the centurion to pronounce, "Surely this man was the Son of God"? (What finally moved you to that realization?)

RESPOND AND GROW

(16:14-18)   How does the risen Jesus both scold and encourage the disciples? What commission does Jesus assign to His disciples and to us? How will you "preach the gospel" in your world today?

What idea, verse, or phrase can change my experience today?

_____

_____

_____

Jesus as Ideal Man

The centurion, seeing what had happened, praised God and said, "Surely this was a righteous man" (Luke 23:47).

THE GOSPEL ACCORDING TO LUKE

- To whom is salvation available? I'm not a Jew by birth.
- Can I believe the details of Christ's life?
- What roles do prayer and the Holy Spirit have in my life?

"... it seemed good also to me to write an orderly account for you, most excellent Theophilus, so that you may know the certainty of the things you have been taught" (1:3,4)—and Luke's purpose is just as valid for us twenty centuries later. His gospel stands as one of the high-water marks of New Testament writing. A self-conscious and meticulous historian, as well as a trained physician, Luke hones his literary skills to present a firm historical foundation for faith in Jesus Christ. His biography of Jesus is also an account of the beginning of the life of the church, a history which he continues in the book of Acts.

Luke's gospel is characterized throughout by a strong note of joy—a note which four times breaks into hymns of praise: the *Magnificat* of Mary (1:46-55), the *Benedictus* of Zechariah (1:68-79), the *Gloria In Excelsis* of the angels (2:14), and the *Nunc Dimittis* of Simeon (2:29-32). The source of this joy is Luke's message to the world: God's salvation is available to all people through the death and resurrection of His Son, Jesus Christ.

Luke also emphasizes the importance of prayer and the work of the Holy Spirit. The selection of stories reflects Luke's own warm interest in people—the sick, the helpless, the poor, the social outcasts, the children, and, in a striking way, the women of that day. Two of Luke's favorite phrases are "preach the gospel" and "salvation"—phrases which summarize, respectively, the character of Jesus' ministry and the content of His message. The portrait which Luke paints of Jesus is that of perfect manhood: He is "Son of man" as well as "Son of God."

When you read Luke's account of the life of Jesus, note these elements:

1. The universal relevance of the message of Jesus Christ
2. The joyful tone of praise
3. The perspective and portraits of women
4. The emphasis on prayer as modeled by Jesus' life
5. The sensitivity to a Gentile audience (The genealogy, for instance, goes back to Adam, son of God, rather than to Abraham)
6. Luke's careful work as historian (He cites six datings to establish the time of John the Baptist—Luke 3:1,2)

DAY 15

☐ **Luke 1–3**

READ AND ANSWER

(1:11-20) Consider Zechariah's reaction to the angel's news. Is it irreverent? Understandable? Surprising?

(2:8-20) The shepherds respond to the angels and their message in three stages. What are the three stages? Have you experienced any or all of them? If so, which one(s) and when?

(3:7-18) What is John's message? Describe his approach.

REFLECT AND PRAY

(1:26-38) Think about the issue of an unmarried mother at this time. What do Mary's reactions reveal about her character? When have you had to struggle between having people's approval and submitting to God? Which did you choose? What was the outcome?

RESPOND AND GROW

(1:46-56) Describe the emotions behind Mary's song. Why does she praise God? Which of those reasons can you also praise God for?

What idea, verse, or phrase can change my experience today?

_____

_____

_____

READ AND ANSWER

(4:28-30) Imagine this scene—what kind of emotions would people be feeling? What would the noise level be? How does Jesus handle the excited mob?

(5:12,13) Who asks for healing in this passage? How does Jesus respond? Why would Jesus' touch be significant to a leper? Imagine the inner healing caused by that simple gesture.

REFLECT AND PRAY

(4:1-6) What struggle is going on in these six verses? What does Jesus' example here teach about the value of knowing Scripture? What comfort do you get from reading that Jesus was tempted—just as you are?

RESPOND AND GROW

(4:42; 5:16; 6:12) What significant pattern emerges? Is this a pattern of your life? Should it be? If you think so, start today!

What idea, verse, or phrase can change my experience today?

_____

_____

_____

☐ **Luke 7–9**

READ AND ANSWER

(8:22-25)   What were the disciples feeling as they woke Jesus? What happened to their faith?

(9:46-48)   What do you think Jesus felt when He heard the disciples' argument? Jesus and His disciples have different definitions of greatness. What do the disciples learn here? What does Jesus' teaching mean to you?

REFLECT AND PRAY

(7:41-47)   Why did the woman "who had lived a sinful life" love Jesus so deeply? Why do you love Jesus? Have specific instances of His forgiveness increased your love for Him?

(9:57-62)   What excuses do these people have for not following Jesus? What excuses do you have for not following Him today?

RESPOND AND GROW

(8:19-21)   How does Jesus identify His mother and brothers? Will you look like a mother or brother to Jesus today? In other words, what part of Jesus' teaching will you put into practice today?

What idea, verse, or phrase can change my experience today?

_____

_____

_____

READ AND ANSWER

(10:30-37)   What question is Jesus answering with the story of the Good Samaritan? What is Jesus' answer?

(10:38-42)   How do Martha and Mary respond to Jesus' presence in their home? Which behavior does Jesus commend? Why? (Are you more like Mary or Martha?)

(12:13-21)   According to Jesus, what are right and wrong attitudes toward material possessions?

REFLECT AND PRAY

(11:5-13)   Why does the man give his friend bread? Why does God give us what we request? Is there any reason not to approach God? How certain can you be that He will answer?

RESPOND AND GROW

(11:37-54)   What is Jesus' message when He compares the Pharisees to the cup and dish? What are some modern equivalents to the hypocritical actions and appearances of the Pharisees? Does your inner life correspond to the image you project on Sunday morning?

What idea, verse, or phrase can change my experience today?

_____

_____

_____

☐ **Luke 13–15**

Read And Answer

(13:18-20) What fact about God's kingdom do the parables of the mustard seed and the yeast illustrate?

(14:7-11) What does this story teach about our estimation of ourselves and God's perspective on us? How are we to think of ourselves? When have you been humbled after exalting yourself? When have you been exalted after humbling yourself?

Reflect And Pray

(15:11-31) What is the theme of this parable—and the two which precede it? When have you felt like the elder brother in the story? When have you felt like the younger son (verse 21 especially)? Thank God your Father for His forgiveness and love.

Respond And Grow

(14:12-14) What does Jesus suggest should motivate us to hospitable acts? What often motivates us to entertain in our homes? When did you last invite someone who couldn't repay you to do something with you? Try it today!

What idea, verse, or phrase can change my experience today?

_____

_____

_____

DAY 20

READ AND ANSWER

(17:3,4)   Jesus warns us not to be stumbling blocks for other people. What instruction are we given here? How do you intend to deal with your brother's (or sister's) sins?

(18:1-8)   What motivates the judge to grant the widow's petition for justice? What motivates God to answer our petitions?

REFLECT AND PRAY

(17:11-19)   What does this account of a healing illustrate about human beings? Are you negligent when it comes to thanking God for the ways He blesses you? Spend some time now offering your thanks.

RESPOND AND GROW

(18:35-43)   Why do you think Jesus asks this obvious question? Are you direct in asking God for things? What can you praise God for today?

What idea, verse, or phrase can change my experience today?

_____

_____

_____

☐ **Luke 19–21**

(19:28-44)   What moves Jesus to tears—and what do the tears reveal about His attitude as He speaks of the coming judgment? (Does the state of the world and its impending judgment move you to tears? Why or why not?)

(20:1-8)   Why does Jesus' question silence the people?

(21:5-19)   What signs—political, natural, religious, and personal—will precede the end of the age? How do verses 15 and 19 complement each other?

(21:34-36)   What effect does this warning have on the way you are currently living? What thoughts and feelings come to you when you consider standing "before the Son of Man"?

(20:20-26)   What is the issue here? How do the state and church conflict today? What is your moral obligation in these instances?

What idea, verse, or phrase can change my experience today?

_____

_____

_____

DAY 22

READ AND ANSWER

(22:7-20)   Read the passage again after you read Exodus 12:1-28. How is Jesus Christ the ultimate Passover lamb?

(23:26-43)   Having read two gospels, what is most striking about Luke's account of the crucifixion? What image, personality, or detail stands out?

REFLECT AND PRAY

(22:39-46)   What kinds of feelings does Jesus experience here? What obstacles keep the disciples from praying? What obstacles keep you from praying?

(22:31-34,54-62)   Consider verses 54-62 in light of verses 31-34. Who knows us better—God or we ourselves? What do you think and feel about being known so well by God?

RESPOND AND GROW

(24:1-12)   How would you have responded to this discovery? What would you have said to the disciples? What do you say to people when you want to tell them this same message that Christ is alive today? Who will you talk to today?

What idea, verse, or phrase can change my experience today?

_____

_____

_____

Jesus as the Eternal Son of God

But these are written that you may believe that Jesus is the Christ, the Son of God, and that by believing you may have life in his name (John 20:31).

THE GOSPEL ACCORDING TO JOHN

- Who did Jesus claim to be?
- What did He teach?
- Why should I believe?

John's gospel is a call to faith: His specifically evangelistic purpose is to produce in his listeners faith in Jesus as the Christ and as the Son of God. Consequently, he has chosen those events and teachings which bring into focus the specific claims of Jesus. Written to be understood by the Greek as well as the Jew, John's gospel again and again strikes the keynote of Jesus as Son of God and belief in Him as the source of eternal life.

The ultimate question for faith is, "Who is Jesus?" and John sets up the multi-part answer as he presents seven signs, seven discourses, and seven "I am" statements made by Jesus. An outline of these elements is essentially an outline of the gospel. (See the outline in the Appendix.) More importantly, this outline is a foundation for belief. As you read John's gospel, be sensitive to the urgency of Jesus' ministry: His time on earth is controlled by "the hour" when God's redemptive purpose will be accomplished by the crucifixion (2:4; 4:21,23; 5:25,28; 7:30; 8:30; 12:23,27; 13:1; 17:1).

READ AND ANSWER

(1:1-18) Why did "the Word become flesh"?

(3:16-21) Why did God send His Son into the world?

(3:22-36) What does John teach about Jesus here? Describe your relationship to God's Son.

REFLECT AND PRAY

(2:1-11) What is Jesus' first sign that He is the Christ? What power did His mother expect Him to have? What power do you expect Him to have?

RESPOND AND GROW

(3:1-15) Initially, what does Nicodemus know about Jesus? Even with this knowledge, what must Nicodemus (and you) do to have eternal life? Have you taken that step of belief?

What idea, verse, or phrase can change my experience today?

_____

_____

_____

☐ **John 4–6**

READ AND ANSWER

(4:27-38)   What does Jesus teach here? Why can the reaper and the sower rejoice together?

(5:1-9)   What question does Jesus ask the invalid? Why do you think He asks that question? (Do we always want to be healthy? Consider the responsibility that comes with being spiritually, emotionally, psychologically, or physically strong.)

REFLECT AND PRAY

(6:1-15)   Why does Jesus ask Philip the question of verse 5? What information and comment does Andrew offer? Imagine how Philip and Andrew felt as the events of verses 10-13 unfolded. When have you felt that way?

RESPOND AND GROW

(4:7-26)   Why do the Samaritan woman and Jesus talk? What do they talk about? Contrast Jesus' discussion with this woman and His discussion with Nicodemus. What does this teach us about how to share with others our knowledge of Jesus Christ? Who will you talk to today about Jesus?

What idea, verse, or phrase can change my experience today?

_____

_____

_____

☐ **John 7–9**

READ AND ANSWER

(8:31-36)   What actions show people to be Jesus' disciples? What promise does Jesus make for those who "know the truth"? What are believers set free of?

REFLECT AND PRAY

(9:1-7)   According to Jesus, why is this man blind? What difficult time or sudden tragedy in your life proved to be an opportunity for the work of God to be displayed in your life?

(9:8-34)   Skim this passage again: Note the development of the healed man's testimony. How has the story of your faith become bolder or more specific with time?

RESPOND AND GROW

(7:53–8:11)   Describe the situation. (Look back to 3:17, too.) What does Jesus teach in this passage about judging? How can you apply this principle in your life today?

What idea, verse, or phrase can change my experience today?

_____

_____

_____

DAY 26

☐ **John 10–12**

READ AND ANSWER

(10:1-21)   What "I am" statements does Jesus make in this passage? How does He differentiate between the true and false shepherd? How do the sheep distinguish between the two?

(11:25,26)   What does Jesus' claim in verse 25 mean to you? Answer the question He asks in verse 26.

REFLECT AND PRAY

(12:42,43)   Why didn't some of the Pharisees believe Jesus? When can verse 43 be said about you? In what areas of your life is praise from people more important to you than praise from God?

RESPOND AND GROW

(11:1-6)   When does Jesus go to Lazarus? What does this schedule suggest about the difference between God's timing and our human timing? Complete this sentence: "Today I will let go of my timing in this situation:

_____

and I will see how God works."

What idea, verse, or phrase can change my experience today?

_____

_____

_____

DAY 27

READ AND ANSWER

(13:34)   Consider the context of this command. Who has just left the upper room? What is he planning to do? What standard of love does Jesus establish?

(14:25-31)   What is the connection between the Holy Spirit, the gift of peace, and Christ's return?

REFLECT AND PRAY

(13:36–14;14)   What questions do Peter, Thomas, and Philip have for Jesus? How does Jesus answer these questions? What does John 14:6 mean in your life? Verses 13,14?

(15:5-8)   Identify and explain the relationship between the vine, the vinedresser, and the branches. When have you experienced the withering that comes with separation from the vine? Now how do you "remain" in Jesus Christ?

RESPOND AND GROW

(13:1-17)   Imagine being one of the disciples here. Which would be easier for you—washing someone's feet or having someone (Jesus) wash your feet? Why? What are Jesus' actions here an example of? What will you do today to live according to verse 14?

What idea, verse, or phrase can change my experience today?

_____

_____

_____

☐ **John 16:5-18**

READ AND ANSWER

(16:12-16)   What will the Spirit do when He comes?

(17:20-26)   What does Jesus pray for you, a believer because of the original disciples' message? (See verse 20.)

REFLECT AND PRAY

(16:5-11)   What are three aspects of the work of the Holy Spirit? How does the Holy Spirit work in your life in regard to sin, righteousness, and judgment? Give a specific instance of each.

RESPOND AND GROW

(17:6-19)   What requests does Jesus make for His disciples? What does Jesus mean by a disciple being "in the world" but not "of the world"? Why does Jesus stress the difference? How will your life reflect this distinction today?

What idea, verse, or phrase can change my experience today?

_____

_____

_____

READ AND ANSWER

(19:1-16)   Contrast Pilate's words and actions. What does he say? What does he do? (See 18:38, too.) When do your words and actions match? What do you feel about Pilate—his predicament? His actions?

(19:28-37)   What is Jesus' last statement? What is "it" that has been finished?

REFLECT AND PRAY

(20:24-31)   Explain the connection between seeing and believing for Thomas, for Jesus, and for yourself.

RESPOND AND GROW

(21:11-19)   Why does Jesus ask about Peter's love for Him three times? What actions does Jesus want as a result of Peter's love for Him? What actions result from your love for Jesus? What action will you take today because you love Jesus?

What idea, verse, or phrase can change my experience today?

_____

_____

_____

The Spirit Continues
the Work Jesus Began

Therefore go and make disciples of all nations, baptizing them in the name of the Father and of the Son and of the Holy Spirit, and teaching them to obey everything I have commanded you... (Matthew 28:19,20).

THE ACTS OF THE APOSTLES

- How will I know what to say to unbelievers?
- Will I be bold enough to speak?
- What will characterize my relationships with fellow believers?

In his gospel, Luke offers an orderly account of the life of Jesus and the beginning of the Christian movement in the first-century world. In the book of Acts, Luke covers a period of approximately thirty years from the birth of the church (with the coming of the Holy Spirit at Pentecost) to Paul's imprisonment in Rome. While the "acts" related are mainly those of Peter and Paul, the book might be even more appropriately titled "The Acts of the Holy Spirit." It is His direction and power which enable the work of the apostles and missionaries.

With the same painstaking attention to detail found in his gospel, Luke the historian tells the ongoing story of salvation as it spreads throughout the New Testament world. First, the day of Pentecost marks Jesus Christ's gift of His Spirit to the church: The Holy Spirit would enable the early church—and enables us today—to do its mission of making the gospel known. The command of the resurrected Christ outlines the general movement of the gospel message "in Jerusalem, and in all Judea and Samaria, and to the ends of the earth" (1:8). In the book of Acts, Luke shows that this movement is happening. He tells of the expansion of Christianity with six brief progress reports (6:7; 9:31; 12:24; 16:5; 19:20; 28:31).

Luke's writing also reflects a certain interest in apologetics: He writes to commend Christianity to the Roman government. He carefully points out that Christians were not enemies of the Empire; they were not a menace to law and order. A modern reader can also find in Acts a model of Christian worship and fellowship, as well as inspirational examples of the bold and life-changing witness of everyday people. The unmistakable lesson is this: Despite the opposition encountered by these early respondents to Christ's Great Commission and due to the power they received from the Holy Spirit, "the word of God continued to increase and spread" (12:24).

☐ **Acts 1–3**

READ AND ANSWER

(1:1-11)   What does the risen Christ *teach* about the end times, what *promise* does He extend to believers, and what *assignment* does He give?

(2:14-41)   Outline the main points of Peter's sermon.

(3:11-26)   What does Peter say about the purpose of Jesus' life?

REFLECT AND PRAY

(1:12-26)   What decision needs to be made? How do the disciples make the decision? How can you follow their example in your own life?

RESPOND AND GROW

(2:42-47)   What actions and attitudes characterize this early fellowship? What can you learn from this example and apply to your own fellowship community?

What idea, verse, or phrase can change my experience today?

_____

_____

_____

READ AND ANSWER

(4:1-21)   What five claims does Peter make about Jesus Christ?

(5:33-41)   What angered the Sanhedrin? (What does the "this" of verse 33 refer to?) What strategy does Gamaliel suggest? How do the apostles respond to the beating they receive? (Is this your attitude during difficult times?)

(6:1-7)   What are the qualifications for the new workers described here?

REFLECT AND PRAY

(4:23-31)   What are the different parts of the disciples' prayer? As they pray, do they emphasize circumstances changing or themselves changing? (See verses 29,30.) Do you pray for deliverance from circumstances or for God's help as you deal with them?

RESPOND AND GROW

(4:32-37)   What does the description of the early fellowship model for your own fellowship? What can you learn? What can you imitate?

What idea, verse, or phrase can change my experience today?

_____

_____

_____

DAY 32

☐ **Acts 7-9**

READ AND ANSWER

(8:1-3) Why do the people scatter? What are they to do now in these new locations?

(9:1-18) What key event is described here? How is the "before" and "after" Saul different? (See 7:58 and 8:1-3.)

REFLECT AND PRAY

(8:9-25) What change seems to take place in Simon the sorcerer? Why do the people of Samaria want the Holy Spirit? Why does Simon want this power? Why do you want God's power in your life?

RESPOND AND GROW

(8:26-40) What happens in this passage? Consider Philip's example: Are you able to answer people's questions? Are you always alert for the opportunity to share your faith? Be alert today!

What idea, verse, or phrase can change my experience today?

_____

_____

_____

☐ **Acts 10–12**

READ AND ANSWER

(10:9-33)   What led Peter and Cornelius to come together? What does their meeting teach about the character of God?

(10:34-48)   What is Peter's message? How did his earlier vision contribute to this sermon?

(11:19-30)   Outline the growth of the church. How is God bringing about this expansion?

REFLECT AND PRAY

(11:1-18)   What conflict arises and how does Peter deal with this contention? How does your fellowship group handle such contention?

RESPOND AND GROW

(12:12-17)   What do you think is one item the people were praying about? Describe Rhoda's rather humorous reaction to the knock at the door. When have you been surprised by answered prayer? Make a list of prayer requests now. Pray regularly, noting God's answers.

What idea, verse, or phrase can change my experience today?

_____

_____

_____

DAY 34

☐ **Acts 13–15**

READ AND ANSWER

(13:16-41)   What is the main point of Paul's sermon? What are some facts he shares about Jesus? Why does Paul refer to his message as "good news" (verse 32)?

(13:42-52)   What are the various reactions to Paul's words? Who leads a person to belief in Jesus? (See verse 48.) How do the disciples respond to their missionary efforts? (See verse 52.)

(14:8-20)   What misunderstanding about God becomes evident through the people's behavior? What do Paul and Barnabas explain to these people?

REFLECT AND PRAY

(13:1-3)   Describe the church at Antioch. How is it similar to yours? What things happen at Antioch that don't happen at yours?

RESPOND AND GROW

(15:1-11)   What is the issue here? Why is it important? What conclusion do the apostles and elders come to? Explain in a few sentences what you believe is essential to being a Christian.

What idea, verse, or phrase can change my experience today?

_____

_____

_____

☐ **Acts 16–18**

READ AND ANSWER

(16:25-34)   Why are Paul and Silas in jail and how do they respond to their imprisonment? What influence do you think their conduct had on the jailer's conversion? What kind of witness do you have in difficult circumstances?

(17:16-31)   What props characterize the worship of the Athenians? What issue, therefore, does Paul address? What is Paul's main argument against idolatry? Can the scathing commentary of verse 21 apply to you right now?

REFLECT AND PRAY

(18:9-11)   How does God confirm Paul's work? How does God confirm your work or the direction in which your life is going?

RESPOND AND GROW

(16:6-10)   How does God lead Paul? How does God guide you? Be attuned to His guidance throughout today.

What idea, verse, or phrase can change my experience today?

_____

_____

_____

DAY 36

☐ **Acts 19–21:36**

READ AND ANSWER

(19:8-10)   What does the phrase "the Way" refer to? How does Paul deal with the attitudes and behavior of this group of people?

(19:23-27)   What causes this new wave of opposition? What are the silversmiths most concerned about? What does this concern reveal about their religious convictions?

REFLECT AND PRAY

(21:10-14)   Where is Paul planning to go? (See 19:21; 20:22-24.) How do his friends feel about this plan, and what does Agabus prophesy? How does Paul respond to the prophecy and to the concern of his friends? How do you deal with conflicts between God's will for you and the perspective or advice of friends?

RESPOND AND GROW

(20:18-38)   What does Paul claim as the most important—only important—task of his life? What is the most important purpose or goal in your life? List two or three activities of your day which reflect this purpose.

What idea, verse, or phrase can change my experience today?

_____

_____

_____

DAY 37

READ AND ANSWER

(22:22)   How does the crowd react to Paul's story? Why do you think they responded in this way?

(24:5-27)   What accusations are brought against Paul? How does he answer these charges? Describe Felix. What kind of person does he seem to be? What does he plan to do with Paul?

(25:1-22)   Compare Festus and Felix—their personalities, their actions, and their plans for Paul. How is Paul affecting the government officials he finds himself facing? (Read again 9:15,16.)

REFLECT AND PRAY

(22:30–23:11)   How do the Pharisees and Sadducees differ philosophically? What is Paul's strategy when he faces the Sanhedrin? What special encouragement does God offer Paul? Reflect on a time when God encouraged you in a personal and significant way.

RESPOND AND GROW

(22:2-21)   What does Paul offer as his defense? When and for what purpose do you share your testimony? Who will you talk to today about Jesus?

What idea, verse, or phrase can change my experience today?

_____

_____

_____

☐ **Acts 25:23–28**

READ AND ANSWER

(26:19-31)   Note Paul's climactic closing statement. How does Paul transform trial into witness? Compare the reactions of Agrippa and Festus.

(27:1-44)   Describe the action and danger of this chapter. What are God's messages to Paul? What is the prisoner Paul's role in this sailing venture?

REFLECT AND PRAY

(27:21-26)   How does Paul react to the danger? How do you think he influenced his fellow travelers? How do you tend to respond to dangers and unknowns in your life? What kind of influence does this reaction have on the people—believers and nonbelievers—around you?

RESPOND AND GROW

(28:1-10)   What does Paul do during this unplanned visit to Malta? Do you, like Paul, serve people even when the opportunity unexpectedly interrupts your plans? Give over to God today's tight schedule. Treat interruptions as opportunities to serve.

What idea, verse, or phrase can change my experience today?

_____

_____

_____

Justification by Faith

I am not ashamed of the gospel, because it is the power of God for the salvation of everyone who believes: first for the Jew, then for the Gentile. For in the gospel a righteousness from God is revealed, a righteousness that is by faith from first to last, just as it is written: "The righteous will live by faith" (Romans 1:16,17).

THE LETTER OF PAUL TO THE ROMANS

- Do I really need God?
- What must I do to receive God's forgiveness and the gift of eternal life?
- How will my life reflect my beliefs?

A masterful statement of doctrine and practical instruction, the book of Romans answers the ancient question, "...how can a mortal be righteous before God?" (Job 9:2). The theme of Paul's epistle is that faith in Christ is the only basis upon which we can be accepted by God. Wanting to introduce himself to the church at Rome which he has not yet visited, Paul carefully outlines the fundamental principles of the gospel.

The doctrine of justification by faith alone is the truth which the letter teaches: God lays on me the righteousness of His Son if I believe in Him—He clothes me in Jesus Christ—and He treats me *just as if* I never sinned. In other words, when we have faith in God, He looks at us through Christ and accepts us into His family and into His kingdom of everlasting life. In writing about this, Paul discusses first the principle (chapters 1–11) and then its effect on the life of a believer (chapters 12–16).

DAY 39

☐ **Romans 1–3**

(1:18-32)   What portrait of human beings does Paul paint here? List several adjectives.

(3:9-20)   What is the function or purpose of the law?

REFLECT AND PRAY

(2:17-29)   What hypocrisy does Paul challenge, and what do you think he means by "circumcision of the heart"? What quality of God does Paul emphasize here?

RESPOND AND GROW

(2:1-16)   What are some key differences between God's judgment of us and our judgment of ourselves and others? Consider the basis, perspective, and appropriateness of the judgment. Today work on curbing your tendency to judge and criticize.

What idea, verse, or phrase can change my experience today?

_____

_____

_____

DAY 40

READ AND ANSWER

(4:1-8) Why was Abraham justified?

(5:12-21) What message is Paul sharing in this contrast between Adam and Jesus, law and grace, death and life?

(6:1-14) Now that we believe, what is to be our relationship to (a) sin, (b) Jesus Christ, and (c) life?

REFLECT AND PRAY

(6:15-23) Contrast slavery to sin with slavery to righteousness; evaluate the quality of life and the eventual outcome of both kinds of enslavement.

RESPOND AND GROW

(5:1-11) What reason for joy and what seemingly odd occasion for joy does Paul discuss here? What suffering in your life can you rejoice about today because of this perspective?

What idea, verse, or phrase can change my experience today?

_____

_____

_____

☐ **Romans 7–8**

READ AND ANSWER

(7:7-13) What observation about human nature does Paul offer in this discussion about the way the law can affect our behavior? (See verse 8.)

(8:18-27) What hope for the future (verses 22,23), insights about the nature of hope (verses 24,25), and reasons for hope (verses 26,27) does Paul discuss?

(8:28-39) What is the exultant Paul's message in these 12 verses?

REFLECT AND PRAY

(8:1-17) Describe life in the Spirit, noticing especially the promise, responsibility, and privilege of verse 17. Ask God to fill your life with this Spirit.

RESPOND AND GROW

(7:14-25) Describe Paul's frustration—and comment on whether you ever experience these feelings. Claim God's help as you face this new day.

What idea, verse, or phrase can change my experience today?

_____

_____

_____

☐ **Romans 9–11**

READ AND ANSWER

(9:1-29)   Who are the children of Abraham and how have they responded to God?

(10:5-21)   What is the relationship between confession and belief, and why, therefore, is it important to share the news of Christ?

(11:1-10)   What does Paul explain about God's attitude toward the remnant of Israel and about the gift of God's grace?

REFLECT AND PRAY

(11:11-24)   What does the vine illustration teach about (a) believers' attitudes and (b) the nature of God?

RESPOND AND GROW

(11:25-36)   What thoughts about God prompt Paul's song of praise? Write three or four sentences of your own praise.

What idea, verse, or phrase can change my experience today?

_____

_____

_____

☐ **Romans 12–13**

READ AND ANSWER

(12:1,2)   What kind of conduct does Paul call believers to, and what is the basis for this change?

(13:8-10)   Explain how loving one another is the fulfillment of the law.

REFLECT AND PRAY

(12:3-8)   Evaluate your self-image in light of verse 3, and consider how well you are using one of your spiritual gifts for the body of Christ.

(13:11-14)   How is your "armor of light" obvious in your daily living?

RESPOND AND GROW

(12:9-21)   Choose one of these exhortations and plan specifically how you will act on it during the day.

What idea, verse, or phrase can change my experience today?

_____

_____

_____

DAY 44

READ AND ANSWER

(14:1-8)   What does Paul instruct the Romans—and you—about different religious practices?

(15:1-13)   How is Jesus Christ an example of obedience to verses 1 and 2?

(16:1-27)   What warnings and blessings does Paul leave with his readers?

REFLECT AND PRAY

(14:9-18)   What are some "stumbling blocks" of the twentieth-century world?

RESPOND AND GROW

(14:19-23)   What general guidelines does Paul offer here? How will you live out the charge in verse 19 today? Be specific.

What idea, verse, or phrase can change my experience today?

_____

_____

_____

The Lordship of Christ

*To the church of God in Corinth, to those sanctified in Christ
Jesus and called to be holy, together with all those everywhere
who call on the name of our Lord Jesus Christ—their Lord
and ours...* (1 Corinthians 1:2).

PAUL'S FIRST LETTER TO THE CHURCH AT CORINTH

How can a believer stand strong in a world like this?
- Messengers are greater than the message they proclaim, and rivalry within the church results.
- Human wisdom is valued over God's wisdom; philosophy or science becomes a god.
- Society is characterized by open immorality and values are threatened by the pressures of materialism.

Paul's first letter to the people of Corinth could easily be addressed to believers today who are wrestling with questions about their faith—especially, "How do we live by God's principles in our contemporary world?" What, for instance, is an appropriate role for women in the church? How should Christian love manifest itself in our daily lives? What role should spiritual gifts play in a worship service? How is Christ's resurrection the foundation of our faith?

As if these issues weren't enough for a young church, the Corinthians were also struggling against the influences of a pagan and immoral society. Paul was confronting believers about sexual immorality, lawsuits against one another, marriage and divorce, and a variety of behaviors which could cause other believers to stumble.

To this city notorious for its immoral ways (the term "corinthianize" had come to mean "to live an immoral life"), Paul offers this epistle of reproof and some intensely practical advice about living a life of faith. He writes strong words of correction, encouraging words of the power that God supplies when we are tempted, and inspiring words about love being the greatest of all spiritual gifts. As you read these sixteen chapters, be sensitive to resemblances between the world of Corinth and your own world.

DAY 45

☐ 1 Corinthians 1–4

READ AND ANSWER

(1:10-17)   What had caused the divisions in the Corinthian church?

(1:18–2:5)   In explaining the terms "foolishness of God" and "man's wisdom," summarize the content of Paul's message here—what is he teaching?

(2:6-16)   What is the source of "God's secret wisdom"?

REFLECT AND PRAY

(4:8-13)   What does Paul reveal about his personal circumstances? Imagine the Corinthians' feelings upon hearing these details and consider how you handle difficult times in your life.

RESPOND AND GROW

(3:1-23)   What figures of speech does Paul use to illustrate unity in the church? What one thing can you do this week to promote unity in your church or fellowship group?

What idea, verse, or phrase can change my experience today?

_____

_____

_____

☐ **1 Corinthians 5–7**

READ AND ANSWER

(6:12-20) According to Paul, why is sexual immorality such a serious sin for a believer?

(7:1-40) Summarize Paul's main points about marriage, singleness, relationships with unbelievers, and self-control.

REFLECT AND PRAY

(6:1-11) What instruction does Paul offer regarding lawsuits among believers? What is your opinion of his viewpoint?

(7:32-35) In contrast to these verses, outline some ways that a husband and wife can encourage each other's relationship to God and enhance their devotion and service to Him.

RESPOND AND GROW

(5:1-8) List one of the examples of moral failure which Paul outlines here. Identify the "yeast" which is now interfering with your relationship to God and today work on eliminating it (be it worries, impatience, fear, frustration) from your life.

What idea, verse, or phrase can change my experience today?

_____

_____

_____

DAY 47

READ AND ANSWER

(9:15-27)   What is Paul's attitude toward and strategy for preaching the gospel?

(10:23–11:1)   What are the limitations to our Christian freedom?

REFLECT AND PRAY

(8:1-13)   Why does Paul introduce the discussion of eating food sacrificed to idols with these verses?

(11:17-34)   What does communion mean to Paul? To you?

RESPOND AND GROW

(10:1-13)   What lesson(s) can we learn from Israel's experiences? What situation in your life can verse 13 help you face? Carry that verse with you today!

What idea, verse, or phrase can change my experience today?

_____

_____

_____

DAY 48

☐ **1 Corinthians 12–14**

READ AND ANSWER

(12:1-11)   What is the source and what is the purpose of the spiritual gifts Paul discusses here?

(12:12-31)   What does the reference to the human body teach about the unity and diversity of the various spiritual gifts?

(14:26-40)   What are a few basic guidelines for sharing these gifts?

REFLECT AND PRAY

(13:13)   What is your understanding of the relationship between faith, hope, and love? Why does Paul assert that "the greatest of these is love"?

RESPOND AND GROW

(12:31–13:7)   What is the "most excellent" gift? (Note the context of this discussion of love as it follows the lessons of chapter 12.) Choose one attribute of love to work on today. Ask God to teach you how to love in this way.

What idea, verse, or phrase can change my experience today?

_____

_____

_____

DAY 49

READ AND ANSWER

(15:1-11)   List the details of the gospel message which Paul outlines, noting also how he substantiates his claims.

(15:35-58)   What ideas about our resurrection bodies did you learn from Paul's discussion of a seed, stars, and Adam?

REFLECT AND PRAY

(15:12-19)   Why is the fact of Jesus' resurrection essential to our Christian faith?

RESPOND AND GROW

(15:58; 16:13,14)   Choose a phrase that will be your encouragement through the day. Use it to encourage yourself or someone else.

What idea, verse, or phrase can change my experience today?

_____

_____

_____

Comfort and Ministry

Praise be to the God and Father of our Lord Jesus Christ, the Father of compassion and the God of all comfort, who comforts us in all our troubles, so that we can comfort those in any trouble with the comfort we ourselves have received from God (2 Corinthians 1:3,4).

PAUL'S SECOND LETTER TO THE CHURCH AT CORINTH

- What does God's grace mean in my life?
- How does my accepting Christ change me?
- How am I to be a steward of my money?

Scholars still puzzle over the number of letters Paul wrote to the church at Corinth and the number of visits he made there. Some people feel that Paul wrote a second and more severe letter after the epistle we know as 1 Corinthians failed to bring the people to repentance. The book we refer to as 2 Corinthians, then, would be the third in the sequence. Whether it is second or third, though, the thirteen chapters reflect Paul's joy and relief at the changes in the Corinthian church. The epistle stands as one of the most emotional and personal of Paul's writings.

Paul shares words of great despair and ecstatic joy as he writes of his love and concern for the Corinthian believers. Paul, too, tells of his own sufferings—the danger and disappointment, the hardship and humiliation—which he experiences as he carries out his commission to spread the news of Jesus Christ. Chapters 10–13 contain sharp words in defense of his ministry—a response to hostile Corinthians who have challenged his authority. (This section may be the remaining part of Paul's missing second letter to the church.)

Still, joy and tenderness characterize chapters 1–9. Note the frequent occurrence of the words "comfort" and "ministry." Besides being a spirited defense of his ministry, 2 Corinthians emerges as a pastor's loving attempt to guide his flock to a life of unity and love for one another. Three dominant themes emerge: God's grace is sufficient for all things; people are new creatures in Christ; and Christian giving should be a joyful act of love.

DAY 50

READ AND ANSWER

(1:12–2:4)   List several qualities of Paul that are revealed in these verses. What is striking about his personality?

(2:5-11)   Why is forgiveness important?

REFLECT AND PRAY

(1:3-7)   How can suffering bring us closer to God and to each other?

RESPOND AND GROW

(3:18)   How is God working in your life to transform you into His likeness? At the end of the day, note one way He specifically touched your life today.

What idea, verse, or phrase can change my experience today?

_____

_____

_____

☐ **2 Corinthians 4–6**

(5:1-10)   What is Paul's attitude toward earthly things? Toward heaven?

(6:3-13)   What qualities has Paul exhibited in the midst of the trials he has suffered?

(6:14-18)   Why should believers remain separated from nonbelievers?

REFLECT AND PRAY

(4:4)   What is blinding nonbelievers today? Consider the message of advertising and the media, for instance.

RESPOND AND GROW

(5:17)   List three specific attitudes or actions which reflect the newness of you since you have come to know Christ.

What idea, verse, or phrase can change my experience today?

_____

_____

_____

☐ **2 Corinthians 7–9**

READ AND ANSWER

(7:8-11)   What is the relationship between sorrow and repentance, and what results from genuine repentance?

(8:10-12)   What attitude should accompany giving?

(9:12-15)   What results of giving does Paul outline?

REFLECT AND PRAY

(8:9)   Define the richness and poverty of Christ and your resulting richness which Paul mentions here.

RESPOND AND GROW

(9:6-11)   What promises are made for people who "sow generously" for God's kingdom? Identify one specific thing you can do to "sow generously" today—and then do it!

What idea, verse, or phrase can change my experience today?

_____

_____

_____

DAY 53

□ **2 Corinthians 10–13**

READ AND ANSWER
(10:7-18)   On what basis does Paul boast of his ministry? (Note verse 18.)

(11:23-28)   List the experiences which Paul views as having made him a better servant to God and to the people he pastors. Comment on the list; consider why these experiences were effective "teachers."

REFLECT AND PRAY
(11:13-15)   How does Satan masquerade today?

(12:7-10)   Describe Paul's attitude toward his "thorn," and contrast it with your attitude toward your own trials.

RESPOND AND GROW
(13:5,6)   What self-examination does Paul challenge the Corinthians— and you—to make? How do you rate?

What idea, verse, or phrase can change my experience today?

_____

_____

_____

Freedom in Christ

I do not set aside the grace of God, for if righteousness could be gained through the law, Christ died for nothing! (Galatians 2:21).

THE LETTER OF PAUL TO THE GALATIANS

- What is the doctrine of justification?
- How can I know when I am dealing with a cultic or heretical movement?
- What freedom does a believer find in Christ Jesus?

Written probably ten years before the book of Romans, Paul's letter to the Galatians heralds the same great theme of Christian freedom. This short letter has been called the *Magna Charta* of Christian liberty; Galatians stands as Paul's denunciation of Jewish Christians who attempt to shackle that freedom with the bonds of Jewish legalism (specifically the laws of circumcision and diet). Paul writes about the doctrine of justification by faith. He emphasizes that the inward, spiritual nature of Christianity is quite different from the mere externalism of other religious practices.

Martin Luther offered this description of the book of Galatians: "St. Paul goeth about to establish the doctrine of faith, grace, forgiveness of sins, or Christian righteousness, to the end that we may have a perfect knowledge and difference between Christian righteousness and all other kinds of righteousness." Paul explains that Jesus is sufficient for our salvation whereas cults and other religions wrongly proclaim the message "Jesus plus. . . ."

In developing his thesis, Paul defines the gospel of salvation by grace alone and explains our faith as the proper response to God's grace toward us through the life, death, and resurrection of His Son, Jesus Christ. Paul also discusses the fruit of a life of grace and defends his own ministry. This charter of Christian freedom is strongly worded and carefully argued as Paul offers believers, then and now, the call to be free in Christ.

DAY 54

☐ **Galatians 1–2**

READ AND ANSWER

(1:6-10)   What is Paul's main point in these five verses?

(2:4-10)   What does this passage reveal about Paul's ministry—a controversy he faced, the purpose of his work, and a task he eagerly does?

(2:14-16)   Why can't the observance of the law lead to justification?

REFLECT AND PRAY

(2:17-21)   Explain Paul's assertion that "if righteousness could be gained through the law, Christ died for nothing."

RESPOND AND GROW

(2:20)   How does Christ live in you? What will people see of Christ in you today?

What idea, verse, or phrase can change my experience today?

_____

_____

_____

☐ **Galatians 3–4**

READ AND ANSWER

(3:19-25)   What is the purpose of the law, and how is it related to the promises of God?

(3:26-28)   What does Paul teach about the unity of believers and the basis for that unity?

(3:29–4:7)   Contrast slavery to sin and the law with sonship to God. What freedom and privileges do children of God enjoy?

REFLECT AND PRAY

(3:6-9,15-18)   Who are the children of Abraham—and are you among this number?

RESPOND AND GROW

(4:18a)   What good purpose are you zealous for? How does your life reflect that zealousness?

What idea, verse, or phrase can change my experience today?

_____

_____

_____

□ **Galatians 5–6**

READ AND ANSWER

(5:2-6)   Explain the relationship between circumcision, faith, and love, noting especially the resounding statement that closes this paragraph.

(5:13-26)   What practical limitations does Paul now outline for the Christian freedom he has described?

(6:1-5)   What exhortations to the fellowship and to individual believers within the fellowship does Paul offer here?

REFLECT AND PRAY

(6:7-10)   What is the point of Paul's farming metaphor? What are you now sowing—and what therefore can you expect to reap?

RESPOND AND GROW

(5:22,23)   Consider your life in light of this picture of a believer's life. Choose one characteristic to strive for today, and ask God's assistance.

What idea, verse, or phrase can change my experience today?

_____

_____

_____

The Church: The Body of Christ

And God placed all things under his [Jesus'] feet and appointed him to be head over everything for the church, which is his body, the fullness of him who fills everything in every way (Ephesians 1:22,23).

THE LETTER OF PAUL TO THE EPHESIANS

- Why should I be a member of a church?
- Why is the church so important to God?
- How am I to act as a member of the church—as a member of the body of Christ?

Although modern scholarship has cast doubts on whether the apostle Paul is the author of this letter, conservative scholars accept the epistle as his. In doing so, they credit Paul with writing a definitive statement about the church being the body of Christ and believers being members of that body. Paul uses three figures of speech to describe this mystical community of believers—the temple (2:21,22), the human body (1:22,23; 4:15), and a bride (5:25-32)—but the image of the human body is emphasized.

Paul opens this epistle with words of praise for God's plan to "bring all things in heaven and on earth together under one head, even Christ" (1:10). Despite various backgrounds, races, cultures, or social standings, we are all equal when we accept Jesus Christ. Some critics feel that the wording of this message reads more like a sermon that a pastoral letter. Whatever the original purpose of Ephesians, Paul's wonder at the mystical unity of people in Christ is unmistakable. It is on this theological basis that Paul offers practical instruction about life as a member of Christ's body as well as life in relation to the world. He also addresses the privileges and responsibilities involved in the relationships between husbands and wives, parents and children, masters and slaves: We are to express our oneness in Christ by our everyday relationships with others.

81

□ **Ephesians 1–3**

READ AND ANSWER

(2:1-10)   What does this passage say about the nature of God, the role of Jesus, and the nature of people before and after they know Jesus?

(2:11-18)   How have the Jews and Gentiles been reconciled?

REFLECT AND PRAY

(1:15-23; 3:14-21)   List Paul's prayers for the Ephesians, and model your prayers for your fellowship after this example.

(3:7-13)   What is the purpose of the church? How involved are you in the fulfillment of this purpose?

RESPOND AND GROW

(2:4,5,8,9)   Spend some time thanking God for the grace by which He has saved you, and then carry that thankfulness through your day.

What idea, verse, or phrase can change my experience today?

_____

_____

_____

☐ **Ephesians 4–6**

READ AND ANSWER

(5:21-33)   How is Jesus Christ the model for how wives are to love their husbands? For how husbands are to love their wives?

(4:22–5:7)   Note the contrast between the old self and the new creation in Christ by listing the specific characteristics and behaviors of each.

(6:10-18)   Describe the various pieces of armor and their specific purposes in a believer's battle against the world's darkness.

REFLECT AND PRAY

(5:8-20)   How does Paul define light? How are you this kind of light in your world?

RESPOND AND GROW

(5:1,2a)   How can your life reflect love today? List two specific behaviors for situations you will face.

What idea, verse, or phrase can change my experience today?

_____

_____

_____

Unity at All Costs

Join with others in following my example...I plead with Euodia and I plead with Syntyche to agree with each other in the Lord... (Philippians 3:17 and 4:2).

THE LETTER OF PAUL TO THE PHILIPPIANS

- How can people with different personalities and different opinions work together well in the body of Christ?
- Why is unity important?
- What can I learn from Christ's example?

A simple statistic introduces the tone of Paul's letter to the church at Philippi: The word "joy" or "rejoice" occurs twelve times in the four short chapters. In what has been called a love letter to the Philippians, Paul thanks them for their gifts, tells them of his own situation in prison, explains why he is sending Epaphroditus (the bearer of the people's gift to Paul) back to them, and offers encouragement to these believers who are dear to him.

Paul also addresses the key issue of unity among believers. Having learned of dissension which threatens the peace and usefulness of the church, Paul exhorts the believers to live, act, and witness in the unity of the Holy Spirit. Paul fails to recognize two parties: He instead uses the word "all" again and again throughout the letter. He rejoices that the Philippians are partners with him in spreading the gospel and later urges the fellowship not to be marred by selfishness, pride, or party spirit.

Finally, Paul reveals a glimpse of himself as he writes of his commitment to Jesus Christ and his desire to know Him and make Him known to others. Consider, too, Paul's utter contentment in any circumstance as long as Christ is his strength (4:11-13). Still, the overarching theme is a call to unity. Whereas Ephesians speaks of the church as the body of Christ, Philippians shows how that unity can either be broken or preserved.

DAY 59

READ AND ANSWER

(2:1-4)   List Paul's specific instructions for leading a life of unity.

(2:5-11)   Unity is fostered by the kind of attitude modeled by Christ. Describe that attitude.

REFLECT AND PRAY

(1:12-18)   What are two results of Paul's imprisonment? Do these same things result from your trials?

RESPOND AND GROW

(2:12-18)   What behaviors will make believers "shine like stars"? How will you shine like a star today? Be specific.

What idea, verse, or phrase can change my experience today?

_____

_____

_____

DAY 60

☐ **Philippians 3–4**

READ AND ANSWER

(3:7-14) What is most important to Paul? Why?

(3:18-21) Compare the (a) destiny, (b) god, and (c) glory of the "enemies of the cross" with those of the Philippian believers.

(4:10-13) What is the source of Paul's joy?

REFLECT AND PRAY

(4:4-9) Outline the exhortations Paul shares here and describe the tone of his writing.

RESPOND AND GROW

(4:6) Spend some time in prayer, placing before God those concerns which cause you to be anxious.

What idea, verse, or phrase can change my experience today?

_____

_____

_____

The Supremacy of Christ

See to it that no one takes you captive through hollow and deceptive philosophy, which depends on human tradition and the basic principles of this world rather than on Christ (Colossians 2:8).

THE LETTER OF PAUL TO THE COLOSSIANS

- Is Jesus simply an exceptional teacher, merely a gifted human being?
- How do the gospel teachings about Christ compare with the teachings of the world?
- What is the Christian answer to false teachings about God and Jesus?

Having learned of a threat to the otherwise healthy church at Colossae, Paul writes to the Colossians and attests to the uniqueness and complete sufficiency of Jesus Christ as the Savior of all. Apparently one of several ideas which the Colossians were trying to integrate with their Christianity was a form of gnosticism. (Three other ideas were asceticism, angel worship, and the Jewish rites of circumcision, diet, and festivals.)

The gnostic philosophy deprived Jesus of His unique status as the Son of God by reducing Him to one of a series of divine beings emanating from God. This series of creatures was designed to bridge the gap between the essentially holy God and the essentially evil flesh of human beings. The teaching that Jesus Christ was so emptied of His divinity that He could finally be a man was a dangerous heresy which Paul counters by various proclamations of who Christ is. (See also the introduction to 1 John.)

As Paul outlines this portrait of Christ in all His dignity, deity, and glory, he focuses on the preeminence of Christ as the image of God, the fullness of God, the Creator, and the head of the church. Paul discusses Christ's word as well as Christ's Person: Jesus has freed us from darkness, redeemed us from sin, and reconciled us to God by His blood on the cross. Most importantly, Jesus Christ has become the believer's life (3:4), and so Paul urges us to hold fast to Him.

☐ **Colossians 1–2**

READ AND ANSWER

(1:9-14) What are the specific requests, the purpose, and the attitude of Paul's prayer?

(1:15-23) What is Jesus Christ's relationship to God, to creation, and to you?

REFLECT AND PRAY

(2:9-15,20-23) What impact has the cross had on "the powers and authorities" of the world? On your eternal future? How can this effect on you be evident in your behavior today?

(2:13) Thank God for this act of grace and love.

RESPOND AND GROW

(2:6,7) List some specific ways in which you can be "rooted and built up" in Jesus. What can you do today to "live in Him" and strengthen your faith?

What idea, verse, or phrase can change my experience today?

_____

_____

_____

☐ **Colossians 3–4**

READ AND ANSWER

(3:12-17)   List Paul's exhortations for holy living.

(4:2-6)   What are Paul's instructions for (a) your life and (b) your prayers for your church leaders?

REFLECT AND PRAY

(3:5-11)   What is God's attitude toward these aspects of earthly nature which Paul outlines? What is your attitude? Spend a few moments in silent confession to God.

(3:13)   Ask God to help you see where you need to extend forgiveness to someone and ask Him to help you do it.

RESPOND AND GROW

(3:1-4)   What are some "things above" which you can think about today? Be specific and commit your thought life to God.

What idea, verse, or phrase can change my experience today?

_____

_____

_____

The Coming of the Lord for His People

. . .and to wait for his Son from heaven, whom he raised from the dead—Jesus, who rescues us from the coming wrath (1 Thessalonians 1:10).

PAUL'S FIRST LETTER TO THE THESSALONIANS

- How long are we to wait for Jesus' return?
- How should we live in the meantime?
- What are some details about the Second Coming?

When persecution began following Paul's founding of the church at Thessalonica (Acts 17:1-9), the people sent their beloved missionary away. Upon leaving, Paul remained extremely concerned about the new believers and their existence in the face of stepped-up persecution. When Timothy joined him in Corinth with good news of the Thessalonian church, Paul writes a letter full of joy and relief—and a letter which answers certain questions that had arisen.

First, Paul praises the church for its courage and steadfastness in the face of persecution. He addresses problems—a distrust of the apostle himself, sexual immorality, internal division—and answers questions which were confusing the church: What happens to the person who dies before Christ returns? Why should we work if Christ will be coming back soon? As Paul deals with these specific issues, he writes with the heart of a pastor: He rejoices in the church yet he is concerned about their welfare; he simultaneously thanks God for these people and prays for their needs; he exhorts them to live in a manner worthy of Christ's followers.

DAY 63

READ AND ANSWER

(1:2-10)   How did the people of Thessalonica change when they received the gospel message? Comment, too, on the effect of their faith on other people.

(2:1-6)   What accusations against Paul are implied in his defense?

(2:7-12)   What motives and behaviors characterize Paul, Silas, and Timothy?

REFLECT AND PRAY

(3:7)   When have you been encouraged by another person's faith? Be specific—and be thankful!

RESPOND AND GROW

(2:4)   Can this verse describe you and the way you share your faith? Who will you talk to today about God or Jesus Christ?

What idea, verse, or phrase can change my experience today?

_____

_____

_____

DAY 64

☐ **1 Thessalonians 4–5**

READ AND ANSWER

(4:3-12)   What commendations and exhortations does Paul write to the Thessalonians? In other words, what are they doing right and where can they improve?

(4:13-18)   What question about the resurrection of believers has arisen and how does Paul answer it?

(5:23,24)   How does a believer become holy?

REFLECT AND PRAY

(5:1-11)   Summarize Paul's warning to the Thessalonians and to us.

RESPOND AND GROW

(5:16-18)   Let these verses guide your prayer time now and your behavior throughout the day.

What idea, verse, or phrase can change my experience today?

_____

_____

_____

The Coming of the Lord

. . . This will happen when the Lord Jesus is revealed from heaven in blazing fire with his powerful angels. He will punish those who do not know God and do not obey the gospel of our Lord Jesus (2 Thessalonians 1:7,8).

- What events will precede the Second Coming of Jesus Christ?
- Which is more important—doing my work or watching for signs of the end?

Although the verdict of the scholars is not unanimous, it appears that 2 Thessalonians was written shortly after 1 Thessalonians. This second letter was likely written to reinforce certain teachings and to clarify some misunderstandings which had arisen. These points are prominent in this brief epistle: 1) Paul describes specific events which will precede Christ's Second Coming; 2) he reprimands those who have abandoned their work under the premise that Christians have special privileges; and 3) he warns of undue emphasis on "times and seasons."

Paul again commends the people of Thessalonica for their courage in the face of growing persecution. At the same time, though, he is adamant in his teaching regarding Christ's return—"sudden" does not mean "immediate"—and he exhorts the believers to lead holy and productive lives.

DAY 65

☐ **2 Thessalonians 1–3**

READ AND ANSWER

(1:3-12) What does this passage reveal about the situation of the people at Thessalonica?

(2:1-4, 8-12) What is one sign that will precede the return of Jesus Christ? Note specific details.

(3:6-13) What problem does Paul address here, and how does it relate to misunderstandings about Christ's return?

REFLECT AND PRAY

(3:6,14,15) How should believers act toward these people? What is your opinion of Paul's instruction?

RESPOND AND GROW

(1:3) Write down the words to chapter 1, verse 3. Does this description apply to your life? Make it fit today!

What idea, verse, or phrase can change my experience today?

_____

_____

_____

The Pastoral Epistles

The letters of 1 Timothy, 2 Timothy, and Titus comprise the trio known as the pastoral epistles. Written to individuals rather than to churches, these three letters outline the qualifications and responsibilities of church leaders. The focus is on each person—on one's integrity, on works which illustrate belief, and on conscientious and faithful service to God and His people. These epistles also address the question of how to deal with heretical or rebellious members, thereby emphasizing the importance of doctrinal purity.

The question of authorship is an interesting historical, theological, and linguistic study. Scholars debate whether or not these epistles were edited by a scribe who included fragments of his own work. But we can't say categorically that Paul *didn't* write the letters; therefore, for convenience we will refer to the writer as Paul.

Conduct in God's Household

---

*...you will know how people ought to conduct themselves
in God's household, which is the church of the living God,
the pillar and foundation of the truth* (1 Timothy 3:15).

THE FIRST LETTER TO TIMOTHY

- How are we to deal with false teachers?
- Who is qualified to serve in a leadership position in the church?
- What is the role of good works in my life as a follower of Jesus?

First and 2 Timothy were written to the evangelist Timothy while he was working on the important and difficult assignment of discipling men to become pastors (or congregational leaders). Paul's main advice to Timothy is "avoid"—avoid false teachers and heretical doctrine and preach the gospel of Jesus Christ. Note the instruction for a life of discipleship and the teachings about good works which are still quite relevant twenty centuries later.

READ AND ANSWER

(2:1-6)   What types of prayer does Paul urge and for whom should Timothy and other believers be praying?

(2:8-15)   What do these instructions reveal about Paul's attitude toward worship, its role, and how it should be conducted?

(3:15)   How is conduct in church related to the very purpose of the church?

REFLECT AND PRAY

(1:16)   How is Paul's life an example of Jesus Christ's "unlimited patience" with us? When has He been especially patient with you?

RESPOND AND GROW

(3:1-13)   List the qualifications for overseers (bishops) and deacons. What should you cultivate and eliminate in your life? Choose one thing to focus on today.

What idea, verse, or phrase can change my experience today?

_____

_____

_____

DAY 67

☐ **1 Timothy 4–6**

READ AND ANSWER

(5:3-8)   Summarize Paul's teaching on family responsibility.

(6:6-10,17-19)   What are Paul's main points about material possessions, money, and right attitudes toward them?

REFLECT AND PRAY

(4:16)   Why is it important that a person's life mirrors his doctrine?

(6:1,2)   Consider your attitude toward your employer in light of these verses. What does Paul caution people who work for a fellow believer?

RESPOND AND GROW

(4:8)   Are you working as hard to be spiritually fit as you are to be physically fit? Outline your workout plan for spiritual fitness.

What idea, verse, or phrase can change my experience today?

_____

_____

_____

Victorious Faith

Do your best to present yourself to God as one approved, a workman who does not need to be ashamed and who correctly handles the word of truth (2 Timothy 2:15).

THE SECOND LETTER TO TIMOTHY

- Can faith survive in the midst of persecution?
- Are we to keep preaching even when we suffer for doing so?

This intensely personal letter seems to be written by an imprisoned and lonely Paul. Finding himself deserted by friends and desperately longing for Christian companionship, Paul shares with Timothy these final and strikingly emotional words. These words are Paul's triumphant statements of faith—which are strong despite his persecution and suffering. He also encourages believers to endure suffering and to entrust the gospel message to faithful teachers.

☐ **2 Timothy 1–4**

READ AND ANSWER

(2:3-6)   How do the references to the soldier, the athlete, and the farmer relate to a worker for the kingdom of God?

(2:22-26; 4:2-5)   What qualities are important in a true and godly teacher?

(3:14-17)   What does Paul teach about the importance of Scripture, its purpose, its usefulness, and a believer's responsibility?

REFLECT AND PRAY

(3:1-9)   What evidence of godlessness as outlined here do you see in the world today?

RESPOND AND GROW

(2:15)   How are you sharpening your skills with the tool of God's Word of truth? What will you do today?

What idea, verse, or phrase can change my experience today?

_____

_____

_____

Christian Truth

---

*. . . he saved us, not because of righteous things we had done,
but because of his mercy* (Titus 3:5).

THE LETTER TO TITUS

- What are the basics of Christian truth?
- Who can serve as elder or bishop?
- What kind of life should a Christian worker lead?

Like the pastoral epistles to Timothy, the letter to Titus addresses church organization, false teaching, and immoral conduct. Paul offers Titus instruction about the post of elder or bishop. He exhorts Titus and the people he leads to take a stand against false teaching and to live a life which reinforces their Christian belief.

☐ **Titus 1–3**

READ AND ANSWER

(2:2-8)   List the four groups Paul mentions here. What should be taught to each group?

(2:1,11,12)   What general guidelines for good teaching does Paul offer?

(2:11-14)   How does this doctrinal statement relate to the specific instructions of verses 1-10?

REFLECT AND PRAY

(3:4-8)   Review Paul's summary of the gospel. How do the three persons of the Trinity work together?

RESPOND AND GROW

(3:4,5)   What are some specific details about spiritual rebirth and renewal you've experienced because of God's mercy and the work of the Holy Spirit?

What idea, verse, or phrase can change my experience today?

_____

_____

_____

Practice of Christian Forgiveness

So if you consider me a partner, welcome him as you would welcome me (Philemon 17).

- What actions correspond to words of forgiveness?
- What words can encourage forgiveness?

The only example of Paul's private correspondence that has been preserved, this epistle to Philemon reveals not only the character of its author but is also an illustration of Christian forgiveness. While in prison, Paul had befriended Onesimus, Philemon's run-away slave. Although Paul had come to love this young man and had influenced his conversion to Christianity, he knew that Onesimus was Philemon's lawful slave.

In writing to Philemon, Paul asks for leniency in Philemon's dealings with Onesimus—a man who is returning a different person than the one who had fled (apparently with the aid of his master's money). Onesimus is now a brother in Christ, and Paul urges Philemon to accept him as such. (Paul doesn't plead for Philemon to free Onesimus, but verses 16 and 17 more than hint at this.) Note what is revealed of Paul's character in his plea for Onesimus and the tact and wisdom with which he states his case.

☐ **Philemon**

READ AND ANSWER
(verses 8,9)   Consider how Paul deals with this situation. What option did he forgo and what option did he choose?

(verses 15,16)   How does Paul work within the system of slavery and yet undermine it at the same time?

(verses 8-22)   Which of Paul's personality traits are highlighted in his management of the situation?

REFLECT AND PRAY
(verse 17)   What does this verse teach about degrees of forgiveness? In other words, how does true forgiveness manifest itself in the wronged person's life?

RESPOND AND GROW
(verse 6)   How has actively sharing your faith helped you have a better understanding "of every good thing we have in Christ"?

What idea, verse, or phrase can change my experience today?

_____

_____

_____

Christ's Work for Our Salvation

But the ministry Jesus has received is as superior to theirs [the Old Testament priests] as the covenant of which he is mediator is superior to the old one, and it is founded on better promises (Hebrews 8:6).

THE EPISTLE TO THE HEBREWS

- What do the Old Testament teachings of the Hebrew nation say about Jesus, the One who claims to be the Messiah?
- Since the events of Jesus' life, death, and resurrection, what is the significance of the Old Testament laws, sacrifices, and priests?
- How am I to serve Jesus, the superior priest?

Although questions surround the origin of this epistle—neither author, intended recipient, date, or place of origin can be identified with certainty—it stands as an eloquent defense of the Christian faith, especially its superiority to Judaism. Apparently addressed to a group of Christian Jews wavering between their Jewish heritage and their newfound Christianity, Hebrews states the case for Christianity by showing it to be the fulfillment of the old religion.

The writer of Hebrews compares and contrasts Jesus and His achievements with the priesthood and sacrificial system of the Old Testament. The writer concludes that Jesus Christ is superior to prophets and angels, to Moses and Joshua, and to the Aaronic priesthood. Jesus Christ is the perfect priest who offers the perfect sacrifice—Himself on the cross. Jesus removed once and for all the barrier of sin that stood between God and man and so enables people to enjoy fellowship with God.

As you read Hebrews, notice the great roll call of heroes of the Christian faith, the writer's emphasis on the humanity of Jesus, and the exhortations and warnings regarding Christian living (which are interspersed between sections of exposition and teaching). Note, too, the persistent tone as the writer urges his readers to commit themselves to Christ: Turning back to the inferior substitute of Judaism would cost them their very lives.

DAY 71

READ AND ANSWER

(1:1-9,13)   Summarize the reasons and evidence for Jesus Christ's superiority over the angels. Consider His relationship to God, His power, and His eternal life.

(2:1-4)   What does the writer warn about here?

(2:9,14-17)   Why did Jesus have to become human, suffer, and die?

REFLECT AND PRAY

(2:10-13)   What was accomplished by Jesus Christ sharing our humanity? Be sure to describe your new relationship to Him.

RESPOND AND GROW

(2:18)   Spend some time in prayer asking for Jesus' help as you face various temptations or trials.

What idea, verse, or phrase can change my experience today?

_____

_____

_____

☐ **Hebrews 3–4:13**

READ AND ANSWER

(3:1-6) What is the point of the house? In answering this question, identify the discussion of the house.

(4:1,2) Hearing the message of Jesus needs to be combined with another action if it is to provide the way to salvation. What is that other action?

REFLECT AND PRAY

(3:12,13) Why does sin harden a person's heart?

(4:12,13) What do these verses reveal about (a) God's nature and (b) His knowledge and evaluation of us?

RESPOND AND GROW

(4:12) Ask your loving God to show you those thoughts and attitudes which you need to purge from your heart. Ask His assistance in this cleansing.

What idea, verse, or phrase can change my experience today?

_____

_____

_____

☐ **Hebrews 4:14–7:28**

READ AND ANSWER

(4:14–5:10)   What makes Jesus (a) an especially compassionate priest and (b) a totally effective priest?

(5:11–6:3)   What problem does the writer address here? Where are the Hebrews erring?

(7:13-28)
List Jesus' qualifications for the priesthood and some unique aspects of His priesthood.

REFLECT AND PRAY

(7:11-28)   Summarize how Jesus Christ is superior to Aaron, Melchizedek, and all other priests. How is hope in Jesus superior to hope in the law that defined the priesthood?

RESPOND AND GROW

(4:16)   Act according to this exhortation. Seek God's grace and mercy as you confess your sins and share your needs.

What idea, verse, or phrase can change my experience today?

_____

_____

_____

☐ **Hebrews 8–10**

(8:6,7)   Based on these verses, what is the main point of this section of Hebrews?

(9:11-15,24-28)   How is Jesus Christ's sacrifice of Himself superior to the first covenant?

(10:26-31,35-39)   Why doesn't Christ's perfect sacrifice allow us complete freedom to sin?

REFLECT AND PRAY

(10:1-3,11-14)   Compare the effectiveness of the priests' sacrifices and Christ's offering of Himself.

RESPOND AND GROW

(8:3a)   Thank Jesus Christ, the superior priest, for the sacrifice He made of Himself on your behalf and for the gifts of salvation and eternal life He has given you.

What idea, verse, or phrase can change my experience today?

_____
_____
_____

DAY 75

READ AND ANSWER

(11:1-12,17-40)   What is the relationship between faith and action? In your opinion, which example of faith listed here is most striking? Why?

(12:14-17; 13:1-10)   What is the purpose of these instructions for daily living?

REFLECT AND PRAY

(12:1-3)   Which sin "easily entangles" you? What encouragement does the author of Hebrews offer?

(12:4-13)   How do you benefit from God's discipline? Consider both the necessity and the purpose of your heavenly Father's disciplinary actions.

RESPOND AND GROW

(11:1)   Where is your faith being tested right now? Share your dreams and doubts with God.

What idea, verse, or phrase can change my experience today?

_____

_____

_____

Faith and Works

As the body without the spirit is dead, so faith without deeds is dead (James 2:26).

THE LETTER OF JAMES

- Isn't it enough that I believe in Jesus Christ?
- How can I stand strong against the influences of the world?
- Why do I say things that are hurtful—things that I don't really mean?

As soon as we receive the Christian message, we are to live the Christian life—such is the basis of James' letter. True faith in Christ always spills over into the rest of life: James' call to us to be doers of the Word will be obeyed as a natural result of our faith in Jesus and our relationship with Him. Furthermore, the assertion that faith is alive only when it is evident in works complements rather than contradicts Paul's teaching. While Paul teaches that works of the law cannot bring salvation—only faith can—James teaches that this saving faith must necessarily manifest itself in deeds—without deeds there is no faith.

On this foundation that faith without works is dead, James constructs a manual of faith. He instructs his readers on the issues of charity, chastity, curbing anger, taming the tongue, withholding judgment, managing material wealth, and swearing. When followed, these specific bits of practical advice can help a believer resist the devil and draw near to God: This is an epistle of holy living.

DAY 76

READ AND ANSWER

(1:1-4,12-18) Outline James' teaching about trials (a proper attitude and some positive results) and temptations (their source and his warning).

(2:14-26) What is the relationship between faith and works? What image does James use to illustrate this point?

(3:1-6) List the three examples James lists here and explain the point they teach about the tongue.

REFLECT AND PRAY

(1:5-8) Summarize James' teaching about prayer, and evaluate your prayers in light of his words.

RESPOND AND GROW

(1:22-25) What is the meaning of the discussion of the mirror? What will be the result of your listening to the Word today?

What idea, verse, or phrase can change my experience today?

_____

_____

_____

DAY 77

☐ **James 3:13–5:20**

(4:7-10) Why is humility an important trait for a believer to exhibit? How is Jesus the ultimate example of humility?

(4:13-17) How should believers qualify the plans they make? Why?

(5:7-12) What does James say about patience—the circumstances that call for it, an example we've been given, and encouragement for our own attempts to be patient?

REFLECT AND PRAY

(4:2,3) What teaching about prayer does James reinforce here?

RESPOND AND GROW

(4:4-6) How does friendship with the world contradict your Christian faith in your life?

What idea, verse, or phrase can change my experience today?

_____

_____

_____

Suffering Patiently and Joyously to the Glory of God

Therefore, since Christ suffered in his body, arm yourselves also with the same attitude, because he who has suffered in his body is done with sin (1 Peter 4:1).

THE FIRST LETTER OF PETER

- How can my faith in Jesus help me cope with trials?
- What example does Jesus give me for dealing with hard times?

In this epistle, Peter is a practical theologian: His letter abounds in Christian doctrine, but his epistle contains doctrine related to life. Written to Christians who are suffering under some kind of persecution (the "painful trial" of 4:12), Peter's message is one of comfort, hope, and encouragement to stand firm in their faith in Jesus. Peter also reminds his readers that Christ Himself is an example of how to face suffering and that God the Father is sovereign and therefore trustworthy even during difficult times. Peter adds that the unseen Christ is never far away, that believers will share the glory of His reappearance, and that the expectation of His return should call His people to holy living.

DAY 78

☐ **1 Peter 1–3:7**

READ AND ANSWER

(1:1-12) Describe the attitudes toward the living hope available in Jesus Christ: What are the attitudes of the prophets and angels and what should your attitude be?

(1:3-16; 1:22–2:2) What evidence of faith does Peter expect to find in a believer's life?

(2:13-25) How did Christ model submission and endurance under unjust suffering? What can believers accomplish by their respectful submission to civil authorities? What blessings do believers receive because of Christ's submission and suffering?

REFLECT AND PRAY

(2:9-12) Note the description of believers as a "chosen people." What is your message and your example to the world?

RESPOND AND GROW

(2:17) Plan specific ways to obey this four-part command today.

What idea, verse, or phrase can change my experience today?

_____

_____

_____

DAY 79

READ AND ANSWER

(4:7-11)   Outline Peter's instruction regarding the appropriate attitude for prayer and hospitality, the purpose of love, the use of gifts, and the godly way to speak and serve.

(4:12-17)   What attitude and outlook characterize godly suffering? What results when a person suffers for being a believer?

(5:8-11)   What promise for faithful believers closes Peter's letter?

REFLECT AND PRAY

(3:8,9)   To what have believers been called? To what end?

RESPOND AND GROW

(3:15)   Can you explain "the reason for the hope that you have"? If not, what can you do to gain the necessary knowledge?

What idea, verse, or phrase can change my experience today?

_____

_____

_____

Remembrance

. . . he has given us his very great and precious promises, so that through them you may participate in the divine nature and escape the corruption in the world caused by evil desires (2 Peter 1:4).

THE SECOND LETTER OF PETER

- How can I arm myself against false teachings?
- What is the nature of true knowledge?
- Why has Jesus not yet returned?

Although the authorship of this brief epistle has been widely debated, the value of its message is undeniable. Peter warns Christians of false teachers and their corrupt and corrupting doctrines. The theme, therefore, is true knowledge of the Lord and faithful remembrance of God, His nature, and His promises. As in 1 Peter, readers are called to a practical holiness and to live with the awareness that the Day of the Lord is coming.

In light of these points, the writer of 2 Peter asserts that believers must stand strong against false doctrine and the destruction that it can cause. While 1 Peter addresses the issue of persecution by enemies and offers consolation in the face of suffering, 2 Peter warns believers to beware of the darkness of false teachings which can lead to sinful living. The writer of 2 Peter, therefore, reminds his readers of the truth of the gospel.

READ AND ANSWER

(1:3-9)   For what reason should believers strive for the qualities listed here? List the qualities. Comment on the ordering of these attributes and on their value to the person possessing them.

(1:16-21)   On what grounds does Peter defend his ministry?

REFLECT AND PRAY

(2:20,21)   Why would Peter make this statement? Do you agree or disagree with him?

(3:8-13)   What does Peter explain about God's understanding of time? How does that idea explain something about the seeming delay of Jesus' return?

RESPOND AND GROW

(3:14)   What efforts are you making? What will you do today?

What idea, verse, or phrase can change my experience today?

_____

_____

_____

Know God and Enjoy Fellowship with Him

We proclaim to you what we have seen and heard, so that you also may have fellowship with us. And our fellowship is with the Father and with his Son, Jesus Christ (1 John 1:3).

THE FIRST LETTER OF JOHN

- What kind of fellowship does God want us to experience with Him and with other believers?
- How can a believer walk in the light of God?

While John's gospel was written to bring people to faith (John 20:31), his first epistle is intended to renew faith that has been shaken by false teaching. The heresy John is battling is gnosticism: This sect, claiming to have a superior knowledge of God, looked down on those who adhered to the gospel. The gnostic philosophy that spirit is pure and material is evil led to their denial of Christ's humanity. God being good could have nothing to do with evil matter; therefore, He could not have been incarnate in Christ. In this letter, John clearly teaches that this viewpoint cuts out the very heart of the gospel: If Christ did not become man and die for human sin, there is no Christian faith. (See also the introduction to Colossians.)

As the apostle John counters this heresy, he also writes about what it means to live as a Christian: Knowledge of God and fellowship with Him will be evident in righteousness of life, brotherly love, and faith in Jesus as God incarnate. The three topics of love, sin, and new birth are foundational to this epistle. Note, too, the frequent occurrence of the word "know" or its equivalent and the writer's use of various contrasts (light with darkness or love of the world versus love for God, for instance). Finally, John calls believers to walk in the light of God's commandments. We do this by loving one another, for God is love.

DAY 81

READ AND ANSWER

(1:8–2:2)   Summarize the important promise of these verses.

(3:1-3)   What moves John to praise God here?

(2:5,6; 3:7-10)   What distinguishes a child of God from a person in Satan's bondage?

REFLECT AND PRAY

(2:15-17)   What three aspects of love of the world does John outline here? How can these things interfere with or completely inhibit one's love for God?

RESPOND AND GROW

(1:5-7; 2:9-11)   Explain John's use of the contrast between light and darkness. What behaviors and attitudes reveal which path a person is walking? How will you look like you're walking on the path of light today?

What idea, verse, or phrase can change my experience today?

_____

_____

_____

☐ **1 John 3:11–5:21**

READ AND ANSWER

(4:7-12)   How does God enable us to love and how did He show us His love?

(4:15-21)   The hymn to love continues: (a) What is the relationship between fear, love, and punishment? (b) Why are we even able to love? (c) Who can rightly be called "liar"? (d) What did Jesus command?

(5:6-12)   How does God, Jesus Christ, and the Holy Spirit bring a person to believe the gospel message?

REFLECT AND PRAY

(5:2-5)   Explain the connection for us between the commandments of God and our love for God.

RESPOND AND GROW

(3:18)   Plan two ways you can love "with actions" today.

What idea, verse, or phrase can change my experience today?

_____

_____

_____

Truth: Receive, Obey, and Cherish It

...because of the truth, which lives in us and will be with us forever (2 John 2).

THE SECOND LETTER OF JOHN

- What is the primary command Jesus gives us to live by?
- What truth can help us stand against false teaching?

Questions surround this little homily on truth and love. The author may be the apostle John or an unknown John; the person addressed may be a particular woman, or the "chosen lady and her children" may be metaphorical for the church. Whatever the interpretation, the letter itself focuses on the essential Christian theme that Jesus commands His followers to love one another.

The letter also picks up the warning of 1 John: Beware of false teachers. The date of the letter seems to indicate the importance of excluding hospitality to anyone whose teaching contradicts the truth of Jesus Christ. Only then could faith survive. As he writes toward this important purpose, the author uses the word "love" four times and "truth" five times in the thirteen verses. He calls believers to stand strong in the truth of Jesus Christ which he defends here.

Hospitality and Leadership

We ought therefore to show hospitality to such men so that we may work together for the truth (3 John 8).

THE THIRD LETTER OF JOHN

- In what practical ways can we love one another?

Like 2 John, this epistle deals with the issue of visiting preachers who, as itinerant evangelists, relied on the hospitality of Christians as they traveled. The situation which the writer (probably the author of 2 John) addresses in this epistle involves two men: the kind and hospitable Gaius, and Diotrephes, the arrogant church official who attacked John's character and refused to receive the travelers John commended to him. Also mentioned is Demetrius, perhaps the writer's messenger, and a man praised by all for his life of truth. This two-part message of the church's duty to welcome fellow believers and the danger of petty dictators arising within the church is grounded in a discussion of truth. Truth is the basis of the writer's love and, according to his exhortation, is to be the foundation of our Christian service.

Keep the Faith!

Keep yourselves in God's love as you wait for the mercy of our Lord Jesus Christ to bring you to eternal life (Jude 21).

THE LETTER OF JUDE

- How can I be strong against false teachers?
- How can I identify false teachers?

This solemn epistle by Jude, "a servant of Jesus Christ and a brother of James" (verse 1), is written to Christians who are threatened by traitors and by people who have rejected the faith but have remained in the church. The author condemns these false teachers for their arrogance and immorality and for their denial of the lordship of Jesus Christ. In light of his contemporary situation, Jude expounds on the danger of apostasy by citing several Old Testament and apocryphal examples of God's judgment on faithless Israelites. Woven into this message that God judges corporate as well as individual wickedness are exhortations to believers to keep believing and to keep living as God has commanded. The closing note is one of praise for God Who can keep His people standing fast.

☐ **2 John, 3 John, Jude**

READ AND ANSWER

(2 John 4-6)   What command is the reader reminded of? How does the writer define "love"?

(2 John 7-11)   What criterion for hospitality is set forth here?

(3 John 11)   What guideline for behavior does the writer offer here?

REFLECT AND PRAY

(Jude 20-23)   How can belonging to a body of believers help a person stand strong against false teachers?

RESPOND AND GROW

(3 John 11)   Who or what will you imitate today?

What idea, verse, or phrase can change my experience today?

_____

_____

_____

Jesus in Triumph and Glory

Write, therefore, what you have seen, what is now and what will take place later (Revelation 1:19).

THE BOOK OF THE REVELATION TO JOHN

- Looking at the state of the world, how can I have hope?
- This fallen world seems locked in the bonds of Satan—what, therefore, will the end of the age mean?

When approaching and interpreting this difficult final book of the New Testament, a reader must consider for whom Revelation was first written. John wrote to encourage early Christians who were facing a devastating persecution by Rome, and the words he shares are intended to convey a message of hope and victory.

John's message, though, is couched in symbols which would mean much to believers and nothing to their persecutors. These symbols as well as other standard characteristics of this apocalyptic writing—references to supernatural events, unearthly creatures, metaphors, pseudonyms, and numbers—make Revelation a puzzle for modern readers. Furthermore, as a poetic and visionary work written in picture-language, Revelation is not to be taken literally; it is not a logical treatise or a strict chronological account. While far from being the straightforward writing that we twentieth-century believers are familar with, Revelation can still offer us the same hope and encouragement that it did its first-century readers.

As John writes in the opening line, this book focuses on "the revelation of Jesus Christ, which God gave him to show his servants what must soon take place" (1:1). Having received this information from an angel Jesus sent him, John writes of "what is now and what will take place later" (1:19)—and what will take place is the return of Jesus Christ, the passing away of the earth, the final defeat of Satan, and the end of sorrow, pain, and tears.

Four main interpretive approaches have been used by people trying to understand this book and its message: 1) the preterist—prophecies refer only to Jesus' day and have therefore already been fulfilled; 2) the historical—the predictions are a preview of history and so are in the process of being fulfilled; 3) the futurist—the visions are relevant to the end of the age rather than to the time of the prophet; and 4) the poetic or spiritual—the writer is describing artistically the sure triumph of God over evil, and therefore, literal or historical interpretation is illegitimate. Different eschatological schemes—premillenial, postmillenial, and amillenial—have also arisen as readers have considered the meaning of this book.

Whatever the choice of interpretive approaches and time frames, the book of Revelation continues to communicate the fact that God is in control of this world, and that Christ is Lord of history. The promise of Revelation is a glorious future for a believer who stands strong: The world *is* in the hands of a faithful and loving God.

READ AND ANSWER

(2:1-7)   For what is the church at Ephesus praised? Explain verse 4; what prompts the call to repentance?

(2:12-17)   For what is the church in Pergamum (a) praised and (b) reprimanded?

REFLECT AND PRAY

(3:7-13)   What commendation does the church in Philadelphia receive? Is your church worthy of a similar commendation?

(3:14-22)   What is the main complaint against the church in Laodicea, and how does verse 19 temper that complaint? Can this complaint be made against your church?

RESPOND AND GROW

(1:8)   What is the significance of Jesus' statement? What hope and encouragement do these words offer you?

What idea, verse, or phrase can change my experience today?

_____

_____

_____

☐ **Revelation 4–6**

READ AND ANSWER

(4:1-11)   Jot down your impressions of heaven. Comment on its colors, images, light, and intensity.

(5:4-6)   Contrast the triumphant Lion of Judah, which John and the Jewish nation had long anticipated, with the Lamb that John describes.

REFLECT AND PRAY

(4:1-11)   What qualities of God does this passage reveal or suggest?

(6:1-8)   What patterns or forces in history do the events of the first four seals suggest? Which of these have you seen in your lifetime?

RESPOND AND GROW

(5:9-14)   What do the three songs teach about God's worthiness? How relevant are these songs to your life? Sing one of them today!

What idea, verse, or phrase can change my experience today?

_____

_____

_____

READ AND ANSWER

(8:6-13)   What is the purpose of the events triggered by the first four trumpets? What is destroyed?

(9:1-19)   Who is affected by the fifth and sixth trumpets, and who is protected from these events of verse 4? (See also 7:1-8.)

(9:20,21)   How does this destruction affect the people who survive?

REFLECT AND PRAY

(7:15-17)   What promises are given to the elders? What aspect of this future is most appealing to you?

RESPOND AND GROW

(8:4)   As you praise God, confess to Him, or ask His help or guidance, imagine your prayers rising to your powerful Father.

What idea, verse, or phrase can change my experience today?

_____

_____

_____

☐ **Revelation 10–12**

READ AND ANSWER

(10:9-11)   Why would the revelation be both sweet and sour?

(10:6)   Why had there been a delay?

(12:7-9,12,17)   Despite its defeat, what does the dragon plan to do?

REFLECT AND PRAY

(12:10-12)   What is the message of this section?

RESPOND AND GROW

(11:17)   Spend some time thanking God for His power in the world and in your life.

What idea, verse, or phrase can change my experience today?

_____

_____

_____

☐ **Revelation 13–15**

READ AND ANSWER

(13:5-8)   Describe the activities and nature of this beast of the sea. Note from whom it gets its power and authority and how people respond to it.

(13:11-17)   How is the work of this second beast related to that of the first, and how do people respond to it?

(14:6-12)   Summarize the angels' messages.

REFLECT AND PRAY

(15:1-8)   What aspects of God does this vision emphasize?

RESPOND AND GROW

(13:18a; 14:12)   Ask God for these things that will strengthen believers during these end times.

What idea, verse, or phrase can change my experience today?

_____

_____

_____

☐ **Revelation 16–18**

(16:1-21)   What aspects of creation are affected by the seven bowls of God's wrath?

(18:11-14)   Why was Babylon a valuable city? Note especially the last item on the list of the cargo the city sold to merchants.

(18:20,24)   Why is there great rejoicing over the fall of Babylon?

(16:7)   When have you seen the truth and justice of God's judgment in your life?

(17:14)   Despite the conflicts and confrontations of Revelation, what does this verse remind us about the ultimate victory? How can your life reflect that victory today?

What idea, verse, or phrase can change my experience today?

_____

_____

_____

DAY 90

READ AND ANSWER

(19:11-21) Describe the appearance and the significant accomplishment of the rider whose name is Faithful and True.

(20:1-3,7-10) Summarize the destiny of Satan as John describes it here.

(21:1-27) Consider the new Jerusalem—the source of its glory and the atmosphere of this beautiful and holy city. Explain verse 22 in light of 1 Kings 6:13.

REFLECT AND PRAY

(20:11-15; 21:27) Who will survive God's judgments?

(22:7-17) What is Jesus' message to a reader of Revelation?

RESPOND AND GROW

(22:13) Spend some time now praising God for His promise of a glorious future and for His faithfulness and love in the meantime.

What idea, verse, or phrase can change my experience today?

_____

_____

_____

APPENDIX
Outlines of New Testament Books

THE GOSPEL ACCORDING TO MATTHEW

Chapter

1-2   The genealogy and birth of Jesus Christ, the Messiah

3-4   The baptism and temptation of Jesus and the beginning of His ministry

5-7   *The Ethics of the Kingdom: The Sermon on the Mount*
    Beatitudes (5:1-12)
    Old and New Law (5:17-6:4)
    Lord's Prayer (6:5-15)
    Anxiety (6:25-34)

8-9   Jesus as Doer of Mighty Works

10   *Jesus and His Kingdom Preachers*
    Calling of disciples (10:1-4)
    Cost of discipleship (10:5-42)

11-12   Claims of Christ—and His Rejection

13   *The Parables of the Kingdom*
    The sower (13:1-23)
    The weeds (13:24-30)
    The mustard seed (13:31,32)
    The yeast (13:33)
    The hidden treasure (13:44)
    The pearl (13:45)
    The net (13:47-50)

14-17   The Founding of the Church
    Feeding five thousand (14:13-21)
    Faith of the Canaanite woman (15:21-28)
    Peter's confession (16:13-20)
    Jesus' death foretold (16:21-28)

18   *Life in the Kingdom Community: The Church*

19-23   Journey to Jerusalem

THE GOSPEL ACCORDING TO MARK

Chapter

Look at what comes before and what follows each of the three Passion predictions (8:31-33; 9:30-32; and 10:32-34).

THE GOSPEL ACCORDING TO LUKE

Chapter

THE GOSPEL ACCORDING TO JOHN

Chapter

1:1-18	Prologue: "The Word became flesh and lived for a while among us" (1:14).
1:19-51	Beginnings
2–12	Jesus' Public Ministry

Sign 1—Wedding at Cana: water into wine (2:1-11)

Discourse 1—Nicodemus: New birth (3:1-21)

Discourse 2—Samaritan woman: water of life (4:1-26)

Sign 2—Healing the official's son (4:43-54)

Sign 3—Healing the lame man (5:1-15)

Discourse 3—Divine Son (5:16-47)

Sign 4—Feeding the five thousand (6:1-15)

Sign 5—Walking on water (6:16-24)

Discourse 4—The bread of life (6:25-59)

I AM THE BREAD OF LIFE (6:35)

Discourse 5—Life-giving Spirit (7:25-44)

Discourse 6—Light of the world (8:12-30)

I AM THE LIGHT OF THE WORLD (8:12)

Sign 6—Healing a man born blind (9:1-12)

Discourse 7—The Good Shepherd (10:1-18)

I AM THE GATE FOR THE SHEEP (10:7)

I AM THE GOOD SHEPHERD (10:11)

Sign 7—Lazarus raised (11:38-44)

I AM THE RESURRECTION AND THE LIFE (11:25)

13–17	The Upper Room Discourses with the Disciples

Footwashing (13:1-17)

A new commandment: Love as I have loved you (13:34)

I AM THE WAY AND THE TRUTH AND THE LIFE (14:6)

I AM THE TRUE VINE (15:1)

The Holy Spirit (15:26–16:16)

The High Priestly Prayer (17:1-26)

18-21	The Passion and the Resurrection

THE ACTS OF THE APOSTLES

Chapter

1–8:3   Jerusalem: The Birth of the Church

Appearance, commission, ascension of the risen Lord (1:1-11)

Pentecost (2:1-13)

The preaching of the apostles (2:14-41; 3:11-26; 4:8-20)

Stephen: witness and martyr (6:8–8:1)

8:4–12:25   Judea, Samaria, Antioch of Syria

Philip in Samaria (8:4-8)

Philip with the Ethiopian official (8:26-40)

The conversion of Saul on the road to Damascus (9:1-19)

Peter (10:1–12:19)

13–28   Paul in the Roman Empire

First missionary tour (13:1–14:28)

The Jerusalem conference (15:1-35)

Second missionary tour (15:36–18:22)

Third missionary tour (18:23–21:16)

Paul, a prisoner in Jerusalem, Caesarea, and Rome (21:17-28:31)

ROMANS

1 CORINTHIANS

2 CORINTHIANS

GALATIANS

EPHESIANS

Chapter

PHILIPPIANS

Chapter

COLOSSIANS

1 THESSALONIANS

Chapter
- 1:1-10   Salutation and Thanksgiving
- 2:1-16   Paul's Defense of His Ministry
  - Paul's work (2:1-12)
  - Their reception (2:13-16)
- 2:17–3:13   Events Since Leaving Thessalonica and Prayer for Reunion
  - Timothy (2:17–3:5)
  - "Good news" of their faith (3:6-13)
- 4:1-12   Living to Please God
  - Exhortation to purity (4:1-8)
  - Exhortation to love and labor (4:9-12)
- 4:13-5:11   The Second Coming of Christ
  - Comfort about believers who sleep (4:13-18)
  - The sudden return of Jesus (5:1-11)
- 5:12-28   Practical Exhortations and Conclusion

2 THESSALONIANS

Chapter
- 1:1,2   Salutation
- 1:3-12   Personal Messages
  - Thanksgiving (1:3,4)
  - Encouragement and prayer (1:5-12)
- 2:1-17   The Second Coming
  - The "man of lawlessness" (2:1-12)
  - Encouragement to stand firm (2:12-17)
- 3:1-15   Exhortations
  - To faithful prayer (3:1-5)
  - To diligent labor (3:6-15)
- 3:16-18   Benediction and Closing

1 TIMOTHY

Chapter

1:1,2 Personal Greetings
1:3-20 Call to Oppose False Teaching
    Unsound doctrine (1:3-11)
    Paul's testimony (1:12-17)
2:1-15 Instruction for the Church
    Exhortation to pray (2:1-8)
    Role of women (2:9-15)
3:1-16 Qualifications for Leaders
    Elders or bishops (3:1-7)
    Deacons (3:8-16)
4:1–6:21 Instructions to Timothy
    Timothy's personal conduct (4:6-16)
    Pastoral responsibilities (5:1–6:2)
    False teachers (6:3-10)
    Charge to Timothy (6:11-16)
    Material possessions (6:17-19)

2 TIMOTHY

Chapter

1:1,2 Personal Greeting
1:3–2:13 Encouragement to Be Faithful
    Thanksgiving for Timothy (1:3-5)
    Call to courage and fidelity (1:6-14; 2:1-13)
2:14-26 Godly Living
3:1–4:8 Warning and Charge
    Warning of coming apostasy (3:1-9)
    The defense of faith in Jesus Christ (3:10-17)
    Charge to preach despite persecution (4:1-8)
4:9-22 Conclusion and Paul's Reaffirmation of His Faith

TITUS

PHILEMON

HEBREWS

JAMES

1 PETER

Chapter

2 PETER

Chapter

1 JOHN

2 JOHN

3 JOHN

JUDE

REVELATION

BIBLIOGRAPHY

Alexander, David and Patricia Alexander, David Fields, Donald Guthrie, Gerald Hughes, I. Howard Marshall, Alan Millard, eds. *Eerdmans' Handbook to the Bible.* Grand Rapids, Michigan: William B. Eerdmans Publishing Company, 1973.

Guthrie, D., J. A. Motyer, A. M. Stribbs, D. J. Wiseman, eds. *The New Bible Commentary: Revised.* Grand Rapids, Michigan: William B. Eerdmans Publishing Company, 1970.

Lee, Robert. *The Outlined Bible.* Grand Rapids, Michigan: Zondervan Publishing House, 1981.

Lindsell, Harold, ed. *Harper Study Bible—The Holy Bible: Revised Standard Version.* Grand Rapids, Michigan: Zondervan Bible Publishers, 1952 and 1946.

Patterson, J. Ben. Lectures in *The Bethel Series.* Irvine, California: Irvine Presbyterian Church, January 1980–June 1981.